The

GREATEST PRESIDENTIAL STORIES NEVER TOLD

ALSO BY RICK BEYER

The Greatest Stories Never Told
The Greatest War Stories Never Told

Collins

An Imprint of HarperCollins*Publishers*

HISTORY *Presents*

The

GREATEST PRESIDENTIAL
STORIES NEVER TOLD

100 *Tales from History to Astonish, Bewilder* & *Stupefy*

by Rick Beyer

Designed by Judith Stagnitto Abbate / Abbate Design

Printed on acid-free paper

Library of Congress Cataloging-in-Publication Data

Beyer, Rick, 1956–
The Greatest presidential stories never told : 100 tales from history to astonish,
bewilder, and stupefy / Rick Beyer. — 1st ed.
p. cm.
Includes bibliographical references
ISBN: 978-0-06-0760182
1. Presidents—United States—Biography—Anecdotes. 2 Presidents—United States—
History—Anecdotes. I. Title.
E176.1.B49   2007
973.09'9—dc22
                                                        2007031131

13 14 15 16   ID/RRD   20 19 18 17 16 15 14 13

For Bobbie and Andy

The presidency is a treasure trove of little-known stories that have the power to surprise and amaze.

Consider: George Washington was one of the country's biggest whiskey distributors, but he *wasn't* our first president. Thomas Jefferson was so unhappy with the Bible that he wrote his own version of the gospels. John Quincy Adams left the White House every morning to go skinny-dipping in the Potomac. Abraham Lincoln once took part in a duel—the broadsword was his weapon of choice. William Henry Harrison was killed by one of his own speeches, while Teddy Roosevelt was saved by one of his. John Tyler's life was saved by song. Lyndon Johnson launched his Washington, D.C., career in a bathroom. Jimmy Carter once sighted a UFO. Jerry Ford helped found one of New York's hottest modeling agencies, and George W. Bush never would have been president but for an Englishman rescued at sea in 1620.

And that's just the beginning.

This is the third in my series of *Greatest Stories Never Told* books, written in conjunction with THE HISTORY CHANNEL. Like the first two, it is filled with the kind of history I love—stories that make you shake your head in wonder and lead you to unexpected discoveries. If you want to find out how "Hail to the Chief" came to be the president's song, why the Oval Office isn't square, which president saved the game of football, and why Washington, D.C., could have been named Hertburn, this is the book for you.

The escapades of presidents, and those surrounding them, offer a rich vein of material for strange and fascinating stories. I found no lack of adrenaline-rush material, either. The pages that follow contain shootings, stabbings, battles, kidnappings, a riot, a hanging, and one case of breaking and entering committed by a future president who would be brought down by the same crime forty years later. There's secret surgery on the high seas and a carriage race through Central Park, with Ulysses S. Grant at the reins. I included a few tales about non-American presidents, too, including one who pulled off the neat trick of attending his own funeral while still alive and well. So there is something for everybody.

Many myths and legends cling to the presidents, and anyone who sails in these waters has to be careful to steer clear of them. Sadly, William

Howard Taft did not originate the seventh-inning stretch, as I once believed he did. That was just one of many tantalizing stories that faded in the harsh light of research. Happily, many equally amazing stories turned out to be absolutely true, such as the tale of the woman who brought down Andrew Jackson's cabinet, the little girl who convinced Lincoln to grow a beard, and the forgotten president who helped launch the world's most popular expression. The stories that made the cut and appear in the book are as true as I know how to make them.

Presidents have always fascinated me. When I was four years old I saw one of JFK's last campaign speeches. In high school I started a lifelong hobby of collecting presidential campaign buttons. I can still remember the first time I visited the White House, as the guest of a presidential aide, and got to peek in the door of an empty Oval Office. The thrill has never worn off. As a radio reporter covering the New Hampshire primary, I had a chance to quiz both Jimmy Carter and Jerry Ford. Through writing this book I have gotten to know the rest of the presidents pretty well too, and found plenty about them to astonish, bewilder, and stupefy. I can only hope that you will be as delighted as I was to discover the stories that follow.

The

GREATEST PRESIDENTIAL STORIES NEVER TOLD

MAN OVERBOARD!

A rescue at sea with a profound impact on three future presidents.

A powerful storm battered the *Mayflower* as it carried the Pilgrims across the Atlantic. The wind and waves were nothing short of ferocious. When a young passenger named John Howland came up on deck, the force of the storm swept him into the sea, where he seemed sure to perish beneath the boiling waves.

Fate was kind to John Howland. He just managed to grab a rope trailing from the ship and hold on for dear life. His head disappeared below the surface, but men on deck hauled up the rope until he was alongside the ship, and then fished him out with a boat hook. "Though he was something ill with it," reported another passenger, "he lived many years after."

By that slender thread hang three presidencies.

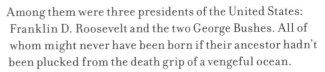

Watching from the deck of the *Mayflower* that day was a twelve-year-old girl named Elizabeth Tilley. She and John Howland eventually married. They populated the New World with ten children, eighty-two grandchildren, and descendants too numerous to count.

Among them were three presidents of the United States: Franklin D. Roosevelt and the two George Bushes. All of whom might never have been born if their ancestor hadn't been plucked from the death grip of a vengeful ocean.

Also descended from John Howland: actors Humphrey Bogart and Alec Baldwin, as well as Joseph Smith, founder of the Church of Latter-day Saints.

A second rescue at sea helped preserve the Bush line. In 1944, Ensign George Bush (in raft, above) was pulled from the Pacific Ocean by crew members of the submarine USS Finback after his torpedo bomber was shot down in 1944.

CUSTODY BATTLE

What if the Father of Our Country had grown up an Englishman?

George Gale married a widow from Virginia and brought her back home to London, along with three children from her previous marriage. But the happy life he envisioned wasn't to be. Not long after they arrived in England, Mildred Gale died in childbirth. Her will directed her new husband to raise his stepchildren, and bequeathed him the money to do so. He dutifully put the two boys, Lawrence and Augustine, into an English boarding school, and applied for legal custody.

The boys were well on their way to being raised as proper Englishmen—until the family of Mildred's first husband back in Virginia decided to dispute the will. A custody battle ensued. It took years to sort out all the issues, but eventually a court ruled that the children should return to Virginia to be raised by relatives there.

That ruling had a dramatic effect on American history.

The name of Mildred's first husband was Lawrence Washington. Her son Augustine, brought back to America from England, eventually had three sons of his own. He named one of them after his stepfather, George Gale.

That boy, of course, was George Washington. The Revolutionary War hero might have wound up serving on the other side, if not for a trans-Atlantic court case.

Imagine the jokes if the name of our most illustrious president (not to mention our capital city) were Hertburn. That was the family name back in 1183, when the king of England gave a knight named William de Hertburn the village of Wessyington in return for his services. De Hertburn changed his name to Wessyington. Through the centuries it morphed into Washington.

THE WAR OF JENKINS' EAR

The oddly named conflict that inspired a presidential landmark.

No war in history has a more striking title than the War of Jenkins' Ear. Robert Jenkins was a British sea captain whose ship was boarded by the Spanish coast guard in the Caribbean. According to Jenkins, the Spanish captain tied him up and cut off his ear with a sword. He was so angry that he brought the severed ear to Parliament, and the prime minister declared war on Spain.

Actually, things were a little more complicated than that. Jenkins didn't exhibit his ear to Parliament until seven years after he said it was cut off. Critics claimed he had lost his ear in a bar fight, and that the whole thing was a political stunt designed to force a war the prime minister didn't really want.

Whatever the truth, England was enraged, and war was waged.

The British hero of this war was Admiral Edward Vernon. Today we remember him less for his exploits, perhaps, than for what he inspired.

One of his officers was a young colonial who owned a farm in Virginia called the Little Hunting Plantation. Lawrence Washington was so impressed with his superior officer that he renamed the farm in Vernon's honor.

Admiral Vernon was known as "Old Grog" because he wore a grogram (grosgrain) cloak in stormy weather. When he diluted the rum ration of his sailors with water, the disgruntled seamen named the watered-down drink after their commander: grog.

When Lawrence died a few years later, his younger brother George inherited the place.

And so it is that America's most famous patriot came to live in a mansion named after a revered British war hero: Mount Vernon, America's only monument to the War of Jenkins' Ear.

Washington took over Mount Vernon upon his brother's death. Over the next twenty-five years he quadrupled the size of the house, turning it into the largest private home in colonial America.

FIRST PRESIDENT

It wasn't who you think.

George Washington is revered as the Father of Our Country. He was not, however, our first president.

Washington was the first president elected under the Constitution, taking office in 1789. But the United States came together as a nation several years before the Constitution was enacted. In 1781, when the last of the thirteen colonies ratified the Articles of Confederation, the new country was officially brought into being.

Shortly thereafter, Congress, by a unanimous vote, made John Hanson the first man elected to a full term as president of the United States. His full title was actually "President of the United States in Congress Assembled." He didn't have all the powers of a modern chief executive, but make no mistake, he was the only president we had. Congress voted to provide the new president with a house and servants, and ruled that he "takes precedence of all and every person in the United States."

Hanson served only a year, and is now largely forgotten, but at the time, a colleague wrote: "I congratulate your Excellency on your appointment to fill the most important seat in the United States."

That letter was signed by none other than George Washington.

Under Hanson's leadership, Congress established the Treasury Department, adopted the Great Seal of the United States (still in use today), and declared the fourth Thursday of every November "a day of Thanksgiving."

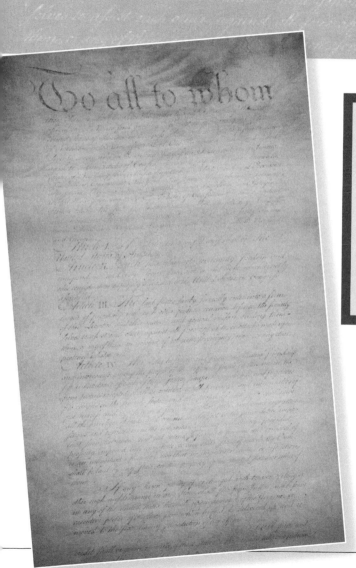

There are other candidates for the title of first president. Some suggest that it was really John Hancock, since he was the first president of the first Continental Congress, before the United States even came into being as a country. Another contender is Samuel Huntington, who was presiding over the Congress when the Articles of Confederation were ratified. But he never used the title and resigned shortly thereafter for health reasons.

The Articles of Confederation were, in effect, the first Constitution. They became the law of the land on March 1, 1781, a date that could be considered the country's birthday. They were in effect for nearly eight years, a period of time often forgotten in American history.

BIBLE BLUNDER

Unscripted moments from the first inaugural.

The very first inauguration of a U.S. president took place not in Washington (which didn't exist yet) or Philadelphia, but at Federal Hall in New York City. The date was April 30, 1789. Organizers had painstakingly planned every detail—or so they thought. Crowds had gathered and George Washington's carriage was already on the way before it occurred to them that something was missing.

Nobody had thought to bring a Bible the new president could use to take his oath of office.

A quick search of Federal Hall failed to turn up a copy of the good book. That's when New York chancellor Robert Livingston, who was to administer the oath, took matters into hand. Like Washington, Livingston was a high-ranking Freemason. He knew there would be a Bible at the nearby Saint John's Masonic Lodge, and dispatched parade marshal Jacob Morton—who was the master of the lodge—to fetch the Bible and rush it back for the swearing-in. The Masonic Bible was opened to a random page from Genesis and Washington placed his hand on it as Livingston administered the oath.

After reciting the oath of office, President Washington added the unscripted words "so help me God," a practice that has been followed by almost every president since.

The Bible, now known as the Washington Bible, has been used by four other presidents for their inaugurations. A fifth, George W. Bush, had to scrap plans to use the Bible because of bad weather. The book was also used at Washington's funeral, the dedication of the Washington Monument in 1885, and the rededication of the U.S. Capitol cornerstone in 1959.

Only one elected president has not used a Bible at his inauguration. Franklin Pierce placed his hand on a law book instead. Pierce was suffering a crisis in faith after the death of his eleven-year-old son in a train accident on the way to Washington for the inaugural. And he didn't "swear" to the oath; instead, he "affirmed" it.

Warren Harding, Dwight Eisenhower, Jimmy Carter, and George H. W. Bush also used the Washington Bible at their inaugurations.

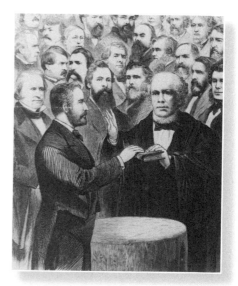

The Washington Bible is still in the possession of Saint John's Lodge. When it travels to an inauguration or some other exhibition, it is accompanied by three members of the lodge, and special arrangements are made so it won't have to go through X-ray machines at airports.

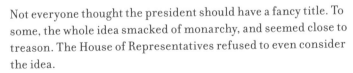

TITLE TRAUMA

What's in a name?

After George Washington was inaugurated in 1789, the U.S. Senate convened in New York's Federal Hall for an important piece of business that took up nearly a month of heated debate. The issue: how to refer to the president.

Many people, Vice President John Adams foremost among them, thought that referring to Washington as "president" simply wasn't enough. "Fire brigades and cricket clubs have presidents," he exclaimed in disgust. Adams argued that it was important to give the highest office in the land a title with more "dignity and splendor."

Others agreed. South Carolina senator Ralph Izard proposed calling the president "His Excellency." George Washington initially favored the title "His High Mightiness." A Senate committee appointed to consider the issue came back with this mouthful: "His Highness the President of the United States of America and Protector of the Rights of Same."

Not everyone thought the president should have a fancy title. To some, the whole idea smacked of monarchy, and seemed close to treason. The House of Representatives refused to even consider the idea.

In the end, the Senate declared that while "it would be proper to annex a respectable title to the office," it would drop the idea to preserve harmony with the House. For Washington and other future leaders of the United States, being called "Mr. President" would have to suffice.

Tongue firmly planted in his cheek, Ben Franklin put forward a suggested title for the vice president: "His Superfluous Excellency."

John Adams was mocked by his enemies for pushing the Senate to give the president an appropriate title. "Our Vice President may go and dream about titles," said Senator William Maclay, "for none will he get."

HOUSE HUNTING

In our nation of immigrants, even the White House is imported.

I n Dublin, Ireland, sits a palace built for the duke of Leinster that is now the home of the Irish Parliament. American tourists can be forgiven if they think it looks familiar.

That's because it was used as a model for the White House.

In 1792, Thomas Jefferson convinced George Washington that the government should hold a competition to pick a design for the president's house. In March of 1792, ads were printed offering "500 dollars or a medal of that value" to the person who submitted the winning design.

The winner was James Hoban, an Irish-born architect from South Carolina. Having studied architecture in Dublin, Hoban was very familiar with the Leinster House. He had also met with Washington, and knew Leinster House was just the kind of building Washington favored—something grand enough for a president, but unpretentious enough to suit a democracy. He probably even showed the president a drawing of Leinster House that had recently been published in a book. The design he submitted closely followed the lines of the Irish building.

Nine designs were submitted. Washington made it clear that he favored Hoban, and his plan was pronounced the winner.

So it is that the building in which American presidents reside reflects the noble tastes of an Irish duke, the egalitarian philosophy of our first president, and the architect who brought them together.

Hoban's design for the White House

Leinster House in Dublin

Hoban's first design was for a four-story building almost identical to Leinster House. Congress balked at the projected expense, so he cut it down in size to the three-story building there now.

> "A GREAT STONE HOUSE, BIG ENOUGH FOR TWO EMPERORS, ONE POPE AND THE GRAND LAMA IN THE BARGAIN."
>
> —JEFFERSON'S DESCRIPTION OF THE WHITE HOUSE AS IT WAS BUILT

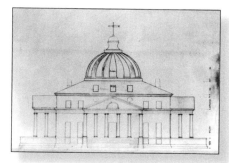
Another of the designs for the White House submitted in the competition is believed by many to be the work of Thomas Jefferson. It is simply signed A.Z.

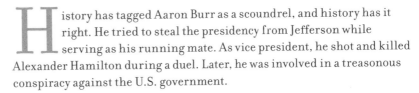

MATCHMAKER

When Jimmy met Dolley.

History has tagged Aaron Burr as a scoundrel, and history has it right. He tried to steal the presidency from Jefferson while serving as his running mate. As vice president, he shot and killed Alexander Hamilton during a duel. Later, he was involved in a treasonous conspiracy against the U.S. government.

But he did make one positive contribution to the country and the presidency. It came in the form of matchmaking.

Burr served as a senator from New York when the nation's capital was still in Philadelphia. When in town he often stayed at Mary Payne's boardinghouse. There he met her widowed daughter Dorothea.

Like many, Burr was charmed by Dorothea's vivacious personality. Had the two become romantically involved, history might have turned out very differently. Instead, Burr introduced her to a friend, a shy Virginia congressman who was still a bachelor at age forty-two.

James Madison.

That's how Dorothea "Dolley" Payne became Dolley Madison, the legendary First Lady who won over Washington and the world with her charm and pluck.

It never would have happened but for a scoundrel.

James Madison couldn't come close to matching his wife's popularity. Charles Pinckney, his opponent for the White House in 1808, put it this way: "I was beaten by Mr. and Mrs. Madison. I might have had a better chance if I faced Mr. Madison alone."

Dolley's finest moment came in 1814, with British troops marching on the White House. She desperately wanted to save Gilbert Stuart's famous portrait of Washington, the one that now appears on the one-dollar bill. When it proved too difficult to unscrew the eight-foot frame from the wall, she coolly ordered the glass broken and the canvas taken out. She escaped only minutes before the British arrived.

A bigger-than-life First Lady, Dolley was famous for her wonderful parties and her amazing gowns. She played cards for money, used rouge, and wore fancy jewelry— all shocking in her day. She lived into her eighties and was personally acquainted with every single president from Washington to Zachary Taylor.

When Dolley died in 1849, President Taylor said, "She will never be forgotten because she was truly our First Lady for a half-century." In 1911, a popular play was written about her, entitled *Dolley Madison: First Lady of the Land.* That's how the term came into general use as a description of the president's wife.

WASHINGTON'S WHISKEY

First in war, first in peace, and first in making the drinks.

George Washington earned distinction as a general and a president. But few realize that he was also one of the colonies' most prolific whiskey manufacturers.

After serving two terms as president, Washington returned to Mount Vernon in 1797. He was eager to find ways to make his farm generate profits, and built the distillery at the urging of his farm manager. Washington considered liquor "essential to the health of men" and apparently considered his distillery essential to the financial health of Mount Vernon.

An archaeological dig of the site suggests it was one of the largest distilleries in the colonies. Six slaves handled the large amounts of grain and water needed to make the whiskey. The distillery featured more than fifty mash tubs and five stills. "I make no use of Barley," wrote Washington. "Rye, chiefly, and Indian Corn . . . compose the materials from which the whiskey is made."

In just one year, 1799, the distillery at Mount Vernon turned out eleven thousand gallons of rye whiskey and earned a profit of $7,500. "The demand for this article [in these parts] is brisk," commented Washington with satisfaction.

So here's to George Washington. He could not tell a lie, but he sure could make that rye.

> **IF THIS DISTILLERY PRODUCES POISON FOR MEN, IT OFFERS IN RETURN THE MOST DELICATE AND THE MOST SUCCULENT FEED FOR PIGS . . . THEY CAN HARDLY DRAG THEIR BIG BELLIES ON THE GROUND.**
>
> —A POLISH VISITOR TO MOUNT VERNON COMMENTING ON HOW THE BY-PRODUCTS FROM THE DISTILLING PROCESS (KNOWN AS STILLAGE) KEPT 150 PIGS WELL FED

After Washington's death, his distillery was sold. It ceased operation in 1807 and was eventually torn down. A replica has recently been reconstructed on the site at Mount Vernon.

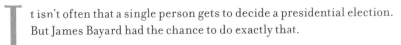

PIVOTAL VOTE

The presidential election that came down to one man.

I
t isn't often that a single person gets to decide a presidential election. But James Bayard had the chance to do exactly that.

The bitter election of 1800 pitted incumbent John Adams against Thomas Jefferson. When the voting was done, Jefferson had defeated Adams. But due to a quirk in the way the Electoral College operated at the time, he was tied with his own vice presidential candidate, Aaron Burr.

That's when things really started to get out of hand. The election went to the House of Representatives. Federalists, who had supported Adams, so hated Jefferson that they decided to throw their support to his vice presidential candidate. And once Aaron Burr realized he had a shot at the top office, ambition took over and he began to maneuver for votes.

The rules required the House to vote by state. On the first ballot Jefferson had eight states—one short of what he needed. Six states went for Burr and two were tied. Over the next few days the House went through thirty-two more ballots. The vote totals remained unchanged.

Tensions were rising. Jefferson supporters threatened to take up arms if he wasn't elected. As President Adams later wrote, "a civil war was expected."

The sole congressman from Delaware, John Bayard controlled that state's vote. The Federalist had been supporting Burr, but after three days of voting he announced he was going to abstain, which would throw the election to Jefferson. Other Federalists stood up and shouted, "Traitor, traitor," at him, but Bayard said he acted to save the country. The deadlock was broken—and Thomas Jefferson became president.

Aaron Burr was a divisive figure. One Federalist who refused to support him under any circumstances was Alexander Hamilton, who called Burr "the most unfit man in the U.S. for the office of President." In 1804 Burr killed Hamilton in a duel.

The building in which the House met was a hardly recognizable, incomplete version of the sprawling Capitol we know today.

The threat of violence was so real that the governor of Virginia, a Jefferson supporter, placed guards around a supply of four thousand arms so that the Federalists would not be able to get their hands on them.

JEFFERSON HANDSHAKE

A radical idea that may have been Thomas Jefferson's greatest gift to politicians.

Thomas Jefferson, the revolutionary genius who wrote the Declaration of Independence, was one of the United States' most gifted presidents. But his passion for equality may best be revealed by a simple gesture. With it, the leader who helped create a democracy in the era of kings and aristocrats set an example for all presidents to follow.

When President George Washington greeted guests at official functions, he bowed stiffly to them, and they bowed in return. The second president, John Adams, continued the custom.

But on the Fourth of July 1801, President Jefferson shocked guests at a White House reception by doing the unthinkable. Rather than bow to his

visitors, he shook their hands. Furthermore, he introduced the practice of treating every guest the same way, regardless of social standing. Even high-ranking diplomats who felt their social position demanded a formal bow had to settle for a simple shake.

Scandalous.

From that day forth, presidents have seized the egalitarian gesture of shaking hands as their own, pressing the flesh at every opportunity. Where would presidential politics be without it?

On New Year's Day 1907, 8,150 people lined up at the White House to shake Theodore Roosevelt's hand. That's a presidential handshaking record that stands to this day. TR's powerful handshake was legendary. "It is a very full and firm grip," wrote one person who shook hands with Roosevelt, "that might bring a woman to her knees."

President Jimmy Carter shook hands with the author of this book when he visited the White House as a radio reporter in 1979.

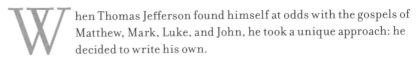

THE GOSPEL ACCORDING TO THOMAS

A presidential rewrite of the Bible.

When Thomas Jefferson found himself at odds with the gospels of Matthew, Mark, Luke, and John, he took a unique approach: he decided to write his own.

Jefferson valued the ethical teachings of Jesus, but he didn't buy into what he called the "corruption of Christianity." He thought the New Testament gospels were filled with material that shouldn't be there. So he cut and pasted the original gospels of the New Testament to create his own version.

It is known today as the Jefferson Bible.

The Jesus of this book performs no miracles. He does not proclaim himself the Son of God. And he does not rise to heaven after dying on the cross. Jefferson thought all these things had been added through the "stupidity" or "roguery" of Jesus' disciples. Jefferson's Jesus was a man, spiritual and prayerful, but simply a man.

Jefferson did the work at night during the first term of his presidency. He hid his radical rewriting of the Bible from the public because he thought it might arouse great controversy. "I not only write nothing on religion," he told a friend; "I rarely permit myself to speak on it."

Jefferson succeeded in keeping his views under wraps during his lifetime. The Jefferson Bible wasn't published until seventy-five years after the president's death.

A spiritual freethinker, Jefferson was vehement in his defense of religious freedom. "It does me no injury for my neighbor to say there are twenty gods or no gods," he wrote. "It neither picks my pocket nor breaks my leg."

Jefferson's pasted-together gospel consists largely of the teachings of Jesus, as told in parables and sermons. Jefferson considered Jesus a philosopher—and was bold enough to point out where his own philosophy differed. "I am a Materialist; he takes the side of Spiritualism," he wrote.

POLITICAL MONSTER

A vice president whose name really went down in history.

Many vice presidents are quickly forgotten. One has been remembered for more than two hundred years because his name became a permanent part of the American language.

In 1812, Elbridge Gerry was governor of Massachusetts. He signed into law a redistricting bill that rearranged state Senate districts in such a way as to give the Jeffersonian Republicans a huge advantage over the Federalists.

One district in particular was stretched into a tortuous shape in order to make sure that a majority of its voters were Jeffersonian Republicans. Federalists howled that it was an abuse of power. Political observers joked that the odd-shaped district looked like a salamander. Engraver Elkanah Tisdale seized on that idea, added claws, wings, and fangs, and published a cartoon in the *Boston Gazette* showing the monster that Gerry created.

The Gerrymander.

While the redistricting kept Republicans in power, many in Massachusetts were outraged, and the political backlash swept Gerry out of office later in the year. But Republicans appreciated his efforts, and he was picked to run as vice president with James Madison.

Now when anyone tinkers with redistricting to give an unfair advantage to one party, it's called gerrymandering. And Elbridge Gerry is remembered one more time.

Gerry was the second vice president to serve under Madison, the first being George Clinton. Oddly enough, both died in office, making Madison the only president to lose two VPs in two terms.

JACKSON AND BENTON

A presidential adviser with a most unusual résumé.

One of President Andrew Jackson's most trusted advisers was Missouri senator Thomas Hart Benton. Pretty extraordinary, considering that twenty years earlier, Benton and his brother had put a bullet into Jackson!

Benton was an aide to General Jackson during the War of 1812, but the two men quarreled over an obscure point of honor. Jackson was fiercely jealous of his reputation, and had already killed one man who had insulted him. One day in Nashville he saw Benton and his brother and went after them with his pistol. It was Jackson, however, who ended up being shot twice and nearly killed.

From that moment on Benton knew that if he stayed in Tennessee, Jackson's friends would exact their revenge. "I am in the middle of hell, and see no alternative but to kill or be killed," he wrote. But he did find an alternative—he lit out for Missouri.

By the time Jackson came to Washington in the 1820s, Benton had become a powerful senator from the "Show Me State." Some thought "Old Hickory" might shoot Benton on sight. But instead he made peace and gained an ally. Together the two men fought attempts to split the Union asunder.

Twenty years after the shooting, doctors finally removed the bullet. Jackson supposedly offered it to Benton saying it was his property. Benton declined, saying that by carrying it for nearly twenty years, Jackson had earned the right to keep it.

Benton is considered one of the great figures in the history of the U.S. Senate, where he served for thirty years. The voters of Missouri eventually ousted him because of his uncompromising stand against slavery.

Tangling with Jackson could be fatal. In May of 1806, Charles Dickinson published a statement in a Nashville newspaper calling Jackson a "worthless scoundrel . . . a poltroon and a coward." Jackson challenged Dickinson to a duel, even though Dickinson was known as one of the best shots in Tennessee. When the two men met, Dickinson fired the first shot, which broke two of Jackson's ribs and lodged near his heart. The wounded Jackson coolly took aim and fired back, killing Dickinson outright.

A CAPITAL IDEA

The only American president to have a foreign capital named after him.

In the early 1800s, James Monroe was one of many people who thought the best solution to the problem of slavery was to remove blacks from the United States entirely.

In December of 1816, Monroe and others founded the American Colonization Society. Its goal was to form a new colony in Africa and encourage free blacks in America to emigrate there.

Some of the people who founded the society were idealists who thought blacks would be happier in Africa. Others were slave owners who considered free blacks troublemakers and wanted to get rid of them. "Of all classes of our population," said Speaker of the House Henry Clay, another founder of the organization, "the most vicious is that of the free colored."

Shortly after the society was formed, Monroe became president of the United States, and used his new position to support the effort. He secured $100,000 from Congress, and the colony of Liberia was founded in 1822. In honor of Monroe's efforts, the capital city was named after him.

It was called Monrovia.

In all, thirteen thousand free blacks were transported to Liberia, but the idea of colonization never really caught on. Today Monrovia is a city of five hundred thousand that recalls a president's failed effort to solve a problem that would one day plunge the United States into civil war.

Joseph Jenkins Roberts was a free black born in Norfolk, Virginia, who emigrated to Liberia with his family in 1828. He became the colony's first black governor in 1841, and Liberia's first president in 1847. Eight Virginians have become president of the United States, and three became president of Liberia.

MAP OF
LIBERIA.

The society bought land for the colony from an African tribal chief for five hundred bars of tobacco, three barrels of rum, five casks of powder, and five umbrellas, among other items.

Colonization was highly controversial among both blacks and whites. Shortly after formation of the society, three thousand free blacks protested against it in Philadelphia. Abolitionists loudly condemned the idea in the 1830s. On the other hand, many saw it as the only answer to the problem of race relations in America. Abraham Lincoln was a big supporter of colonization, and tried in vain to promote it during the Civil War.

THE NAKED PRESIDENT

Adventures with the clothing-optional chief executive.

In looks as well as personality, John Quincy Adams was one of the most straitlaced presidents ever to live in the White House. He was also the only one who liked to stroll down to the Potomac River every morning to go skinny-dipping.

Many in official Washington were unofficially aware of the president's buff-bathing habit. New York political leader Thurlow Weed wanted to see one of the sunrise swims for himself. He secretly observed the president leaving the White House one morning before daybreak. Adams began to shed his clothes before he even got to the river, tied them in a bundle, and jumped in. Thurlow added: "He seemed as much at ease in that element as on Terra Firma."

Another memorable morning, Adams varied the routine. He had a servant named Antoine row him across the Potomac in an old boat, planning to swim back. When a sudden squall blew up, the leaky boat capsized in the middle of the river, dumping both men overboard. They managed to swim to the opposite bank, but Antoine had lost all of his clothes, and the fifty-eight-year-old president was exhausted by the ordeal. Adams gave his clothes to Antoine and sent him to fetch a carriage. Meantime, according to his diary, the president got in some "naked basking on the bank."

Adams referred to the incident as "a humiliating lesson." His wife called it "altogether ridiculous." And while the skinny-dipping continued, the president never tried to swim the entire river again.

WHILE STRUGGLING FOR LIFE, AND GROPING FOR BREATH, [I] HAD AMPLE LEISURE TO REFLECT UPON MY OWN DISCRETION. ”

—JOHN QUINCY ADAMS, COMMENTING ON THE INCIDENT IN HIS DIARY

A crusading female journalist named Anne Royal supposedly bearded Adams during one of his morning swims. As the story goes, she sat on his clothes and refused to leave until he gave her an interview. But neither Adams nor Royal ever mentioned the incident, so while it could have happened, there's no evidence that it did.

DEAD BROKE

*All men are created
equal . . . but some
just can't balance
a checkbook.*

Thomas Jefferson was a man of amazing brilliance and wide-ranging achievement. Not only was he the author of the Declaration of Independence and president of the United States, he was also a philosopher, diplomat, inventor, architect, and musician. Some say he was the most brilliant man ever to reside in the White House. Was there anything this genius couldn't do? The answer is yes.

He was absolutely awful at managing his money.

For his whole life, Jefferson habitually spent more than he took in. Even while making a salary as president *and* earning income from his plantation, he still spent more than he made.

It got him into deep trouble. After his presidency, his debts piled up to astronomic heights. He didn't have enough money to pay for household

items. Things got so desperate that Jefferson persuaded the state of Virginia to pass a special law allowing him to hold a lottery to raise money. He called it "almost a matter of life and death." But few people bought tickets in the Jefferson lottery, and friends started secretly raising money for the former president. Even so, they failed to pay half his debts.

When Jefferson died, on the fiftieth anniversary of Independence Day, his debts exceeded $1 million in today's money. His heirs had to sell his beloved Monticello to pay them off. The man who seemed to be good at everything had died broke.

JEFFERSON LOTTERY.

Register No. Combination Nos.

3 15 31

MANAGERS.
Brockenborough,
Norb. Nicholas,
d Anderson.

Jefferson's daughter Martha was left penniless after his death. She contemplated opening a school to support herself before Virginia and South Carolina each offered her financial support.

JEFFERSON LOTTERY.

Register No. 1979

MANAGERS.
John Brockenborough,
Philip Norb. Nicholas,
Richard Anderson.

Combination Nos. 3 15 31

STATE OF VIRGINIA.

This Ticket will entitle the holder thereof to such prize as may be drawn to its numbers in the JEFFERSON LOTTERY.

Richmond, April, 1826.

For the Managers,

Wm. Grattan, Printer.

When British invaders burned down the Library of Congress in 1814, Jefferson offered his 6,487-volume library as a replacement. Widely seen as a generous gesture, it was actually an attempt to raise some much-needed cash. After a bitter and divisive debate, Congress voted to pay a generous $23,950 to buy Jefferson's books. Recently discovered documents suggest most of the books in the Library of Congress were actually saved from British destruction. Jefferson's friends apparently suppressed that fact so they could distribute a little political pork to the strapped Virginian.

MASONS, MORGAN, AND MURDER

The kidnapping that changed presidential history.

I n 1826, a disgruntled Freemason in Batavia, New York, named William Morgan announced that he was going to write a book disclosing the most sacred secrets of the Freemasons. Local Masons, incensed by Morgan's actions, published advertisements denouncing him and got a friendly sheriff to arrest him for a two-dollar debt.

On the night of September 12, a group of men descended on the jail and spirited Morgan out. "Murder! Murder!" shouted the struggling Morgan as he was thrown into a waiting carriage.

The carriage went clattering into the night, and Morgan was never seen again.

The kidnapping and alleged murder of Morgan triggered a ferocious anti-Mason movement. Clergymen decried the Masons' secret oaths, claiming from the pulpit that Masons were part of an international conspiracy. Hundreds of lodges across the country closed, and the fraternal order's respected position in American society was nearly destroyed.

Before Morgan's kidnapping, Freemasonry had achieved a high degree of public prominence in America. George Washington and Ben Franklin were only two of numerous early American leaders who were Freemasons. But as the order grew in power and influence, people became more suspicious of it.

Out of the emotional protests emerged a new political party, the Anti-Mason Party. It was America's first real third-party movement, and had great success in the Northeast. The Anti-Masons decided to mount a presidential campaign. They gathered in Baltimore to pick a candidate for the 1832 election. In so doing, they became the first political party to hold a national nominating convention. Other parties quickly picked up on the idea. And a new tradition in presidential politics was born.

The Anti-Masons nominated William Wirt (himself a former Mason) as their candidate for president, and presented a platform condemning Masonry for its secrecy and exclusivity. Wirt managed to win one state: Vermont. The victors in the election were two past Masonic grand masters: Andrew Jackson and Henry Clay.

Theories vary on what happened to Morgan. Some believe he was murdered, others that he was driven off to Canada, and still others that the whole thing was a publicity stunt for his book, which was published after his disappearance. The "secrets" it revealed were mostly arcane Masonic rituals. Morgan's wife later became one of the wives of Mormon prophet Joseph Smith.

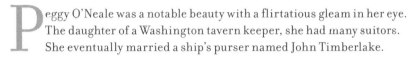

THE PETTICOAT AFFAIR

How one woman brought down the president's entire cabinet.

Peggy O'Neale was a notable beauty with a flirtatious gleam in her eye. The daughter of a Washington tavern keeper, she had many suitors. She eventually married a ship's purser named John Timberlake.

While Timberlake spent a lot of time at sea, Peggy spent a lot of time on the arm of Tennessee senator John Eaton, a boarder at the tavern. Their ten-year "friendship" caused tongues to wag. In 1828, John Timberlake died at sea—some say he committed suicide over his wife's affairs—and John Eaton married Peggy. Washington insiders were indignant. "Eaton has just married his mistress," wrote one politician, "and the mistress of eleven doz. others."

When Andrew Jackson became president he appointed John Eaton secretary of war. The ladies of Washington were scandalized that Peggy would suddenly have a prominent role in Washington society. The wives of cabinet members refused to socialize with the Eatons. Other Washington women followed suit. Soon the Eatons were completely ostracized.

President Jackson was outraged. He hired investigators to refute charges against Peggy, and called a cabinet meeting to defend her. "She is chaste as a virgin," he argued. But members of his cabinet told him they could not force their wives to socialize with Peggy.

Silly as it sounds, the issue polarized Washington and brought business to a standstill. One hundred congressmen threatened to abandon Jackson if it wasn't resolved. Eventually the entire cabinet—including Eaton—had to resign so that Jackson could appoint a new cabinet and business could go forward.

That broke the impasse—and led to a memorable toast: "To the next cabinet: May they all be bachelors—or leave their wives at home."

Peggy Eaton was in her seventies when this photo was taken. "When I was still in pantalets and rolling hoops with other girls, I had the attentions of men, young and old," she said. Even in her later years she was the cause of scandal, marrying her daughter's dancing teacher after her husband died.

66 **DO YOU SUPPOSE THAT I HAVE BEEN SENT HERE BY THE PEOPLE TO CONSULT THE LADIES OF WASHINGTON AS TO THE PROPER PERSONS TO COMPOSE MY CABINET?** 99

—PRESIDENT ANDREW JACKSON, WHEN WARNED THAT MAKING JOHN EATON SECRETARY OF WAR WOULD CAUSE PROBLEMS WITH THE LADIES OF WASHINGTON

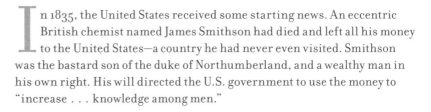

THE BASTARD AND THE BRAHMIN

How an ex-president teamed up with a dead Brit to create an American institution.

In 1835, the United States received some starting news. An eccentric British chemist named James Smithson had died and left all his money to the United States—a country he had never even visited. Smithson was the bastard son of the duke of Northumberland, and a wealthy man in his own right. His will directed the U.S. government to use the money to "increase . . . knowledge among men."

President Andrew Jackson and numerous other American politicians were dubious about accepting a gift from the son of a British nobleman. After all, the British had put Washington to the torch less than twenty years earlier. Senator John Calhoun spoke for many when he said it was "beneath the dignity of the United States to receive presents of this kind."

But one prominent American statesman stood up to advocate acceptance of the gift. Former president John Quincy Adams, scion of the famous Adams family, was now serving as a representative from Massachusetts. Through much of his career, Adams had advocated government support of the arts and sciences. He said the country had "an imperious and indispensable

Smithson had an older half brother, Hugh Percy, the legitimate son of the duke of Northumberland. In one of history's ironies, Percy was a British general who had led troops against America in the early days of the American Revolution. So one brother fought to keep the United States from becoming a country, while the other gave the new country one of its most enduring institutions.

obligation" to put Smithson's money to good use. Adams eventually convinced a reluctant Congress to accept the grant, and spent years making sure it was put to good purpose.

In the end, the gift the United States thought about turning down led to the museum that may be John Quincy Adams's greatest legacy:

The Smithsonian.

Smithson's legacy was about half a million dollars, the equivalent of more than $10 million today. After the money was accepted a ten-year fight took place over how to spend it. Ideas floated included a national university, a botanical garden, and a celestial observatory.

While Congress was arguing over the money, the government invested some of it in a dubious Arkansas land deal. Much of the money was lost to shady operators, but Adams forced the Treasury to replace the funds, thus preserving Smithson's bequest.

125,000 TO ONE

The first-ever attempt on a president's life— and the odds were against him.

House painter Richard Lawrence believed that he was an heir to the British throne and that President Andrew Jackson was trying to keep him from claiming his rightful place among British royalty. So he decided to shoot the president.

Richard Lawrence was extremely crazy. And Andrew Jackson turned out to be unbelievably lucky.

On a gray Friday in January, Jackson attended a funeral service at the U.S. Capitol. Lawrence was waiting behind a pillar as Jackson walked out. The president was just eight feet away when Lawrence pulled a pistol from his pocket and fired at point-blank range.

He was so close he couldn't possibly miss. But the pistol misfired. Much to the horror of everyone present, Lawrence pulled out a second pistol. Jackson was raising his cane at Lawrence and lunging at him, still presenting an easy target. But the second pistol misfired too. A navy officer knocked Lawrence down, and the first-ever assassination attempt on a U.S. president was over.

There was nothing wrong with the pistols. They were loaded correctly. They just didn't go off. It was later estimated that the odds against both pistols misfiring was 125,000 to one.

"Were I inclined to superstition," wrote one friend of Jackson, "the conviction that the President's life was protected by the hand of a special providence would be irresistible."

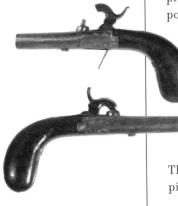

Lawrence used pistols like these in his assassination attempt.

Lawrence was prosecuted by attorney Francis Scott Key, author of "The Star-Spangled Banner." His trial took one day, and the jury took five minutes to find him not guilty by reason of insanity. He spent the last twenty-six years of his life in an asylum.

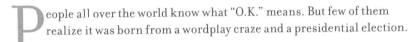

OLD KINDERHOOK

The president who helped launch the world's most popular expression.

People all over the world know what "O.K." means. But few of them realize it was born from a wordplay craze and a presidential election.

It all started in Boston, in 1838. People there started using humorous initials, sometimes combined with purposeful misspellings, just for fun. Newspapers picked up the fad, and writers had a high old time throwing around all sorts of acronyms.

For example:

g.t.d.h.d.	give the devil his due
n.g.	no go
s.p.	small potatoes
O.W.	Oll Wright (all right)
G.T.	Gone to Texas

And there was another expression that started gaining some currency: Oll Korrect, or O.K.

The fad spread quickly to New York, but the phrase "O.K." didn't come into national use until the presidential campaign of 1840. Democrats trying to reelect Martin Van Buren were casting around for political slogans. Van

Van Buren was also known as "the Little Magician" and "the Fox of Kinderhook" because of his political skills. "Kinderhook" is Dutch for "children's corner." Dutch explorer Henry Hudson gave the name to that area of what is now New York in 1609 because he saw Indian children playing there.

Buren was from Kinderhook, New York, and was sometimes called "Old Kinderhook." *O.K.* Political operatives seized on the coincidence. Democrats started forming O.K. clubs and staging O.K. balls. The campaign catapulted the expression into national circulation.

Van Buren lost his bid for reelection. But "O.K." won in a landslide, and is used billions of times a day in all corners of the globe.

A nother theory credits "O.K." to the previous president, Andrew Jackson. It is said that Jackson picked it up from the Choctaw Indian word *okeh,* meaning "That's me" or "That's what I said." There is, however, no evidence to support the idea.

In 1844, James K. Polk also tried to capitalize on the word "O.K."

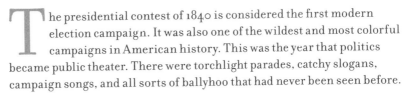

HAVING A BALL

The colorful phrase that rolled in during a presidential campaign.

The presidential contest of 1840 is considered the first modern election campaign. It was also one of the wildest and most colorful campaigns in American history. This was the year that politics became public theater. There were torchlight parades, catchy slogans, campaign songs, and all sorts of ballyhoo that had never been seen before.

The Whig candidate was William Henry Harrison, who back in 1811 had defeated the Shawnee Indians in the battle of Tippecanoe. With his running mate, John Tyler, he boasted one of the most memorable presidential slogans of all time: "Tippecanoe and Tyler Too."

The Whigs seemed to have an inexhaustible supply of campaign gimmicks. One in particular caught on across the country. Supporters in various cities created giant balls, ten feet in diameter, which could be covered in slogans and rolled along in parades. Energetic ball rollers pushed them great distances. One of them was rolled from Cleveland to Akron, another from Kentucky to Maryland, to drum up enthusiasm for Harrison.

"Keep the ball rolling" was the cry of the men who rolled the ball along. "Keep the ball rolling on to Washington."

And so came into our lexicon a phrase still popular today. Harrison rolled into the White House, and we have kept the ball rolling ever since.

Harrison's father, Benjamin Harrison, signed the Declaration of Independence, while his grandson, also named Benjamin Harrison, would follow him to the White House.

Democrats made fun of Harrison as a candidate. One paper said: "Give him a barrel of hard cider and a pension of two thousand a year, and he will sit the remainder of his days in his log cabin." Harrison's campaign team turned it to their advantage, billing him as the "Log Cabin and Hard Cider" candidate.

THE POWER OF SPEECH

One long speech led to a president's death, while another saved a president's life.

On March 4, 1841, William Henry Harrison gave the longest inaugural address any president has ever given. It was more than eight thousand words long and took nearly two hours to deliver.

At age sixty-eight, he was the oldest president yet. To demonstrate that he still had plenty of youthful vigor, he chose to deliver the address without wearing an overcoat or hat to ward off the cold northeast wind blowing in his face.

That turned out to be a big mistake. Weakened by his exposure to the elements, Harrison caught a cold that turned into pneumonia. A month later he was dead.

More than seventy years later, on October 14, 1912, former president Teddy Roosevelt was in Milwaukee running as a third-party candidate to get back into the White House. As he stepped into a car outside his hotel, a man ran out of the crowd and shot him point-blank in the chest.

What saved his life was the fifty-page speech folded up in his breast pocket. It slowed the bullet down enough that it didn't damage any vital organs. Despite the fact that he now had a bullet lodged in his chest, Roosevelt insisted on going to the speaking event to deliver the address that had saved his life.

Secretary of State Daniel Webster, shown standing at the left of the president's deathbed, wrote most of Harrison's lengthy speech. It was designed to convince skeptics that Harrison had what it took to be president. Instead it made John Tyler president.

-1-

Under these circumstances, it has been a matter of genuine regret to me that Senator LaFollette, who has done so much for the Progressive Cause, has felt that because of his antagonism to me he was obliged to range himself against the Progressive Movement in this campaign, thereby giving his old-time enemies, the reactionaries, a much needed support which they have acknowledged by the first praise they have given him in twenty years. It has been asserted that I did not take sides with the LaFollette people in their campaign in Wisconsin in 1904. This is an error. On October 16th, of that year, I made my position clear in a letter to Mr. Cortelyou, Chairman of the National Republican Committee, which ran in part as follows:

"I think Babcock and his people should be told that, especially in view of the decision of the Supreme Court, there must not be any kind

> ## "I SHALL DELIVER THIS SPEECH OR DIE, IT IS ONE THING OR THE OTHER."
>
> —THEODORE ROOSEVELT, INSISTING ON GOING AHEAD WITH THE SPEECH AFTER HE HAD BEEN SHOT

A page of TR's speech with the bullet hole clearly visible

LINCOLN'S DUEL

In which the pen proved a precursor to the sword.

Imagine Abraham Lincoln standing in shirtsleeves, waving a broadsword through the air in preparation for a duel to the death. That was the scene along the Mississippi River on September 22, 1842.

It began when a series of satirical letters appeared in a Springfield newspaper ridiculing state auditor James Shields. The anonymous letters called Shields a "a conceity dunce" and "a fool as well as a liar." They mocked a recent state proclamation he had issued, and heaped insults upon him: "If I were deaf and blind I could tell him by the smell."

The hot-tempered Shields confronted the editor of the paper and demanded to know who had written the letters. The editor quickly pointed the finger at Lincoln.

Shields demanded satisfaction. When Lincoln refused to retract the letters, Shields challenged him to a duel. Lincoln had choice of weapons. "I did not want to kill Shields," he later told a friend, "and I did not want the damned fellow to kill me." Since he towered over Shields, he chose cavalry broadswords, which gave him a huge advantage and underlined the ludicrous nature of the affair.

The antagonists traveled to the dueling ground and were preparing to fight when seconds finally managed to make peace. And what Lincoln referred to as his "scrape with Shields" ended with a handshake instead of a killing.

Many historians believe that Mary Todd wrote several of the letters, and that the normally amicable Lincoln felt he had to stand up for her. Lincoln married Todd just six weeks later.

On his way to the duel, Lincoln reportedly told the story of a soldier whose fiancée stitched the words "Victory or Death" on his belt before battle. He asked her: "Ain't that rather too strong? Suppose you put 'Victory or Be Crippled.'"

The combative Shields, who later served as a general under President Lincoln during the Civil War, is also the only person to serve as a U.S. senator from three states: Illinois, Minnesota, and Missouri.

STATE FUNERAL

Getting a leg up on the opposition.

Santa Anna's funeral was magnificent. A glittering military procession paraded through the streets of Mexico City to the cemetery of Santa Paula. As a large crowd looked on, a crystal urn containing the remains of the Mexican president was placed atop a gilded column. Full military honors were observed. Moving speeches were given.

All in all it was quite a day. Especially given the fact that Santa Anna was alive and well, and in fact stage-managing the entire event.

The funeral was only for his leg.

After losing the Texas War of Independence in 1835, Santa Anna returned to Mexico in disgrace. Three years later, a French fleet attacked Mexico, and Santa Anna leaped into the fray. While rallying the citizens of Vera Cruz against the French, he was struck by a cannonball that took off much of his left leg.

Santa Anna milked his loss for everything it was worth and quickly won back the allegiance of the people. It wasn't long before he was once again president of Mexico. When his popularity started to wane, he ordered the state funeral for his leg.

In the end, its effect was only temporary. Santa Anna soon fell from power, though he would one day be back. As for the leg? Stolen by vandals.

The war in which Santa Anna lost his leg is known as the "Pastry War." A French pastry cook in Mexico claimed his shop had been looted by Mexican soldiers, and appealed to the king of France for help. When Mexico refused to pay damages to the chef, the French used that as an excuse to go to war against Mexico.

In 1847, Santa Anna lost another leg, while fighting an American army at the battle of Cerro Gordo. This time it was his artificial limb, an elaborate affair made of cork, with ball joints at the knee and ankle. Captured by an Illinois regiment, it is displayed today in Springfield, Illinois.

HAIL TO THE WIVES!

The pair of supportive First Ladies who picked a presidential theme song.

After the sudden death of President Harrison, John Tyler became the first vice president to take over at the helm. While some thought he should call himself acting president, Tyler promptly moved into the White House and claimed the title and full powers of the office of president, setting a precedent for later VPs.

The presidency was no picnic for Tyler. People mocked him as "His Accidency." When he vetoed a bill establishing a national bank, almost everyone in his cabinet resigned, his party ejected him, and the first impeachment resolution against a president was introduced in the House.

Tyler's wife died early in his term. Two years later he married a vivacious young woman named Julia Gardiner. After their marriage, they held a series of parties at the White House. The new First Lady, trying to bolster her husband's ego and image, requested that as the president made his entrance at the parties, the Marine Corps Band should strike up a stirring song from a popular stage show.

The name of the song: "Hail to the Chief."

The song happened to be a lifelong favorite of the next First Lady, Sarah Polk. Her husband, President James Polk, did not cut

Julia Tyler

Sarah Polk

a very dashing figure. In fact, he had a way of entering a crowded room almost unnoticed. To help him appear more impressive, she asked that the song be played *every* time he made an entrance. And a tradition was born.

I t wasn't until 1954 that the Defense Department established the song as an official tribute to the president.

music was originally written n English composer in 1812 to mpany a stage production of Sir ter Scott's epic poem "The Lady e Lake." The "chief" in the song Scottish Highlander named erick Dhu, who is eventually d by England's King James.

John Philip Sousa, conductor of the Marine Corps Band, wrote a replacement for "Hail to the Chief" at the request of President Chester A. Arthur, who hated the song. Sousa, composer of such famous marches as "Stars and Stripes Forever," came up with a song called "Presidential Polonaise." Alas, it wasn't one of his great efforts, and failed to make any more of a dent than Arthur's brief presidency.

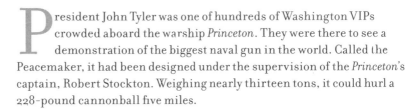

SAVED BY A SONG

When military might threatened the president, a military melody saved him.

President John Tyler was one of hundreds of Washington VIPs crowded aboard the warship *Princeton*. They were there to see a demonstration of the biggest naval gun in the world. Called the Peacemaker, it had been designed under the supervision of the *Princeton*'s captain, Robert Stockton. Weighing nearly thirteen tons, it could hurl a 228-pound cannonball five miles.

After the fearsome cannon was fired twice, the delighted crowd repaired belowdecks for a sumptuous feast. Toasts were drunk and guests began to break out in impromptu song. Then came the announcement: the big gun would be fired one more time. Many hurried up to the deck to get a good view of it.

President Tyler had his foot on the ladder to climb up to the deck when he heard his son-in-law start to sing a military song. It would be rude to leave in the middle of it, so he paused.

That's what saved his life.

Before the song was done, the cannon fired once again. Catastrophe! The gun's breech exploded, sending jagged junks of hot iron flying into the crowd on the ship's deck. Secretary of State Abel Upshur and Navy Secretary Thomas Gilmer were both killed, as were four others.

A navy board of inquiry exonerated Captain Stockton of any blame for the accident. He went on to command the Pacific Fleet and became the first military governor of California. The city of Stockton, California, is named for him.

Among the dead was a friend of Tyler's named David Gardiner. As the fifty-three-year-old president consoled Gardiner's twenty-three-year-old daughter, Julia, in the days following the incident, romance blossomed. The two were married four months later.

President Tyler had another narrow escape after the funeral. Something frightened his carriage horses and they bolted out of control up Pennsylvania Avenue. Near the White House, a man stepped out of the crowd and grabbed the horses, saving the president from possible injury or death.

The Princeton was designed by Swedish designer John Ericsson, who later designed the famous ironclad Monitor. The Princeton was the country's first steam-powered naval ship with a propeller instead of a side wheel.

TELEGRAPH HILL

Presidential politics and the birth of the electronic media.

On May 24, 1844, Samuel Morse sent the first official message over a telegraph line that he had constructed between Washington, D.C., and Baltimore. The message he sent—"What Hath God Wrought?"—is enshrined in history. But at the time it attracted little public notice. Even some of the congressmen who had appropriated money for the venture couldn't see that the thing had much value.

Morse found a way to make the world pay attention to his invention just three days later, when the Democrats opened their political convention in Baltimore. For ballot after ballot, the convention remained deadlocked between presidential candidates Martin Van Buren and Lewis Cass. Morse had his assistant telegraph frequent reports back to Washington.

The age of instant news updates was born.

This was something never before seen. Washington, a city consumed by politics, was transfixed. Crowds began to gather around Morse's telegraph office on Capitol Hill to hear the latest bulletin. According to a Washington newspaper, the *National Intelligencer*, the reports were received "as the responses of the ancient Oracle may be supposed to have been."

The convention went through more than a hundred ballots, with crowds on the Capitol lawn hanging on every vote. Finally the Democrats settled on a surprise candidate, James

James K. Polk

K. Polk. Whatever people felt about the nomination, the *Intelligencer* reported, "there was but one sentiment concerning the telegraph itself, which was that of mingled delight and wonder."

Morse's telegraph was suddenly a big hit. And we've been addicted to instant news ever since.

When Morse sent his now-famous first message between Washington and Baltimore, one of those present was Dolley Madison. He invited her to send the second message, and she gave him one for her cousin in Baltimore: "Message from Mrs. Madison. She sends her love to Mrs. Wethered." So the former First Lady also got to be the first American to send a personal message by telegraph.

> **LITTLE ELSE IS DONE HERE BUT WATCH PROFESSOR MORSE'S BULLETIN FROM BALTIMORE, TO LEARN THE PROGRESS OF DOINGS AT THE CONVENTION.**
>
> —A CORRESPONDENT FOR THE *NEW YORK HERALD*, REPORTING FROM WASHINGTON

MAIL CALL

The mail must go through—unless there's postage due.

I n 1848, the Whig Party held a convention in Philadelphia and nominated General Zachary Taylor as its presidential candidate. Taylor was immensely popular as a result of his victory over Santa Anna in the war on Mexico. He had no experience in politics, no public position on issues, and had never even bothered to vote before, but the Whigs saw him as a sure way to ride to victory.

Whig Party chairman John Moorehead sent a letter to Taylor in Baton Rouge, Louisiana, notifying him of the nomination. Weeks passed, and Taylor made no reply. By this time the news of Taylor's nomination had been in newspapers all over the country. Why wasn't old "Rough and Ready" responding? Didn't he want to be president?

Sure he did. He just didn't want to pay the postage.

In those days, letters were often sent with minimum postage. The expectation was that the recipient would pay the rest. Taylor, as a war hero,

was receiving a huge amount of mail from well-wishers. In an effort to economize, he instructed the postmaster in Baton Rouge not to deliver any mail with postage due.

The letter of notification spent weeks in the dead-letter office before an embarrassed Taylor realized what had happened, retrieved it, and formally accepted the nomination. And the man who Daniel Webster called a "swearing, whiskey drinking, fighting colonel" was on his way to being president.

Taylor's efforts to economize cost him a pretty penny. In the end it cost him $7.50—about $130 in today's money—to retrieve the letter.

Taylor was famous for his unmilitary appearance. He almost never wore a uniform and was utterly lacking in pretension. There are numerous stories about the famous general being mistaken for an old farmer.

" STOP YOUR NONSENSE AND DRINK YOUR WHISKEY. "

—ZACHARY TAYLOR'S RESPONSE WHEN FIRST SUGGESTED
AS A PRESIDENTIAL CANDIDATE. HE LATER WARMED
TO THE IDEA CONSIDERABLY.

SHORT-TERM SOLUTION

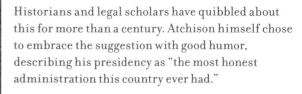

Was David Rice Atchison really president for just one day?

The history books say that President James K. Polk was succeeded by President Zachary Taylor. But there are some who say that there was another president between them, who served as chief executive for exactly one day.

The date in question was Sunday, March 4, 1849. President Polk's term of office officially ended at noon. But because it was a Sunday, Zachary Taylor refused to take the oath of office until the next day.

So who was president from the time Polk's term expired to the time Taylor was sworn in?

Missouri senator David Rice Atchison was serving as president pro tempore of the Senate, which made him next in line after the president and vice president. Therefore, the argument goes, he served as our nation's twelfth president until Taylor's swearing-in.

Historians and legal scholars have quibbled about this for more than a century. Atchison himself chose to embrace the suggestion with good humor, describing his presidency as "the most honest administration this country ever had."

Perhaps he can also lay claim to being the only American president who never made a mistake in office.

A.T. & S.F.

> sked what he did on the day of his
> supposed presidency, Atchison replied:
> "I went to bed." He had presided over the
> Senate in a late-night session the day before.

A.T. & S.F.

Atchison was a senator from Missouri for twelve years, and later became a leader among proslavery Democrats in Kansas before the Civil War. The city of Atchison, Kansas, is named after him.

The president for a day is also memorialized in the name of one of the most famous railroads of all time: the Atchison, Topeka, and Santa Fe.

PATENT PRESIDENT

Yankee ingenuity from a country lawyer.

Many people consider Thomas Jefferson to be the greatest inventor who ever lived in the White House. But Jefferson never bothered to patent any of his ideas. Only one president has ever obtained a patent—someone not normally associated with the cutting edge of technology.

Abraham Lincoln.

In the late 1840s, Lincoln served as a congressman from Illinois. He made part of the journey to and from Washington aboard a Great Lakes steamship. On one occasion, the steamer got stuck on a sandbar. All the passengers and cargo had to be unloaded to float the ship over the sandbar. It was a long and tedious process.

This gave Lincoln an idea: what if there was a way to float the boat over the sandbar without having to empty it out and reload it? When he got back to his law office in Illinois, he began working on a device that would do just that. He whittled the model in between court appearances. The result: patent 6469, "Manner of Buoying Vessels."

Lincoln's invention proved impractical, and was never manufactured. But it did prove that this up-and-coming prairie lawyer possessed a creative mind willing to embrace and act on new ideas—a mind that would be sorely needed by the country in the turbulent years to come.

Lincoln's idea was to add "adjustable buoyant air chambers" below the waterline. When the ship was stuck, these could be filled with air to float it off. It is remarkably similar to the idea that inventors later used to help create the modern submarine.

Among Jefferson's many inventions were a cipher wheel used for encoding messages, a more efficient wooden plow, and this revolving bookstand that could hold five open books at once.

FORGOTTEN FILLMORE

*Remembering a
president that
history left behind.*

Every time we buy a product that's made in Japan—a car, a camera, a digital chip—we would do well to reflect on the overlooked president who made it possible.

Millard Fillmore is perhaps the most obscure chief executive of the United States. He was a little-known ex-congressman when selected as Zachary Taylor's running mate. Taking over after Taylor died in office, the thirteenth president served two and a half years and didn't run for reelection. He is generally remembered for being just another in a series of inept presidents unable to stop the drift toward Civil War.

But Fillmore did one thing that changed the world.

For centuries the Japanese had closed off their country, discouraging trade or any kind of relations with the rest of the world. Fillmore wanted to open up trade with Japan and secure permission for U.S. ships to obtain supplies there. He sent Commodore Matthew Perry and a fleet of warships to force a change.

Perry's mission led to a treaty that established diplomatic relations with Japan. It also made the Japanese realize just how far behind the West they were, and led the country to embark on a crash course of modernization. Japan's subsequent rise to power, first through military might and later through its role as an economic powerhouse, is due in part to the American president almost no one remembers.

Perry brought the Japanese emperor gifts that emphasized the West's technological prowess, including a scale model of a steam locomotive that could travel twenty miles per hour.

> **FILLMORE LACKS PLUCK . . . HE MEANS WELL BUT HE IS TIMID, IRRESOLUTE, UNCERTAIN.**
>
> —HORACE GREELEY

After several other U.S. missions to Japan had failed, Fillmore decided an American show of force was necessary. Commodore Perry sailed into Nagasaki harbor in four steam-powered warships that became known to the Japanese as the "Black Ships." Refused permission to land, he threatened a bombardment. The Japanese realized that they lacked the military power to resist. Perry delivered a letter from President Fillmore, and a treaty followed two years later.

THE FILIBUSTER

The self-made president.

William Walker was an American adventurer who managed to take over another country and make himself president of it—before finding himself in front of a firing squad.

Walker tried being a doctor, a lawyer, and a newspaper editor before turning to something a bit more exciting. He became the greatest of the so-called filibusters: private American citizens with dreams of conquering Central America.

In 1855, he landed in Nicaragua with fifty-seven men he called "the Immortals." He'd been invited there by rebels who were losing a civil war. Astonishingly, he not only became leader of the rebels, he led them to victory. After recruiting other Americans and Nicaraguans to his army, he captured the capital city of Grenada, effectively ending the war.

Walker rigged the election that followed, and got himself installed as president of Nicaragua. The United States quickly recognized his government. Other Central American countries were outraged by what they saw as Yankee imperialism, and united against him. After two years he was forced to flee to the States, where he was greeted as a hero.

In 1860 he returned to Central America with an army of one hundred, dreaming of conquering the whole region. This time he was not so lucky. Captured by the British, he was turned over to the Honduran authorities, who wasted no time in executing him.

Before his adventure in Nicaragua, Walker led a group of rough-and-ready adventurers on an aborted attempt to take over northern Mexico. He proclaimed himself president of the "Lower Republic of California." But eventually the Mexicans chased him and his men back to the border.

The word "filibuster" comes from a Dutch word meaning "freebooter," or pirate. In the U.S. Senate, a filibuster occurs when a small group of senators take over the floor to block legislation.

Walker seemed an unlikely conqueror. He weighed barely a hundred pounds and was incredibly shy. But in battle he turned into a charismatic leader, and he was ruthless in his dealings with those he saw as disloyal.

BUCHANAN'S BLUNDER

The pre–Civil War civil war.

In 1857, President James Buchanan declared the Mormons in the Utah Territory to be in rebellion. There had been a growing conflict over federal jurisdiction in the territory, and Buchanan decided it was time for a show of force. He appointed a new governor and dispatched a force of twenty-five hundred troops to restore order.

When Mormon leader Brigham Young got the word, he began preparing for war. He declared martial law, called up the militia, and began gathering arms. Three years before the Civil War, it looked as if the United States was headed for . . . a civil war.

The American troops that Buchanan sent ran into all sorts of trouble. They got a slow start and ran into fierce winter weather. Mormon raids on their supply wagons forced them to hole up for the winter on starvation rations. Back east, criticism began to mount over how Buchanan was managing things. Newspapers began to refer to the venture as "Buchanan's Blunder." It was proving a huge embarrassment to the administration.

Eventually negotiators worked out a settlement, and conflict was averted. The army entered Salt Lake City peacefully, and the new governor was installed.

Buchanan may have been trying to divert attention from the growing national divide over slavery. Or he may have been trying to show the South that the federal government was prepared to use force to deal with a rebellion. Either way, it didn't work out quite as he planned.

But the expedition cost Buchanan a huge amount of political capital. It crippled his ability to deal with the looming crisis between North and South. When Southern states began to secede, he refused to send troops—perhaps mindful of the criticisms he had borne for the Utah effort.

As a result, the Southern rebellion remained unchecked until Abraham Lincoln took office. It would eventually cost the lives of more than 1 million Americans.

On September 11, 1857, in the midst of escalating tension, 140 settlers from Arkansas traveling through Utah were ambushed and massacred by Indians and Mormons at a place called Mountain Meadow. Twenty years later, a Mormon leader named John D. Lee was hanged for the incident.

A TOUCH OF GRACE

The little girl who remade a president's image.

Norman Bedell was working as a stove maker in Westfield, New York. He was an ardent Republican, and that was enough to make his eleven-year-old daughter, Grace, one as well. One day her dad brought home a campaign poster with a picture of presidential candidate Abraham Lincoln. Grace counted herself a zealous champion of Lincoln's candidacy, but when she peered at her hero she noticed something she didn't like.

Lincoln was clean-shaven.

Beards were growing in popularity, but Lincoln didn't have one. Shortly before the election, Grace sat down and wrote him a letter explaining why he ought to remedy the situation. "All the ladies like whiskers," she wrote, "and they would tease their husbands to vote for you and then you would be President."

A few days later, Grace was astounded to receive a response from the candidate, wondering if whiskers were really a good idea. "Having never worn any, do you not think people might call it a piece of silly affectation should I begin wearing them now?"

This picture was taken on November 25, 1860, less than three weeks after the election. Lincoln's beard is just starting to come in. It was the subject of so much public discussion that the Baltimore Sun *commented: "It is to be hoped there will he no allusions to the important subject of Mr. Lincoln's whiskers in the inaugural address."*

But the little girl's letter struck a chord with Lincoln. After he was elected, he acted on her suggestion and began to grow a beard for the first time in his life. The angular face of the president-to-be was transformed to the bearded visage we know so well today—all thanks to Grace.

The train that carried Lincoln to Washington for his inauguration stopped in Westfield, and Lincoln got out to speak to the assembled crowd. He told them he had "a little correspondent" who had suggested he grow the beard, and asked if she was in the crowd. When Grace was pointed out, Lincoln stepped down from the train platform and made his way toward her. Lincoln kissed the little girl and touched his beard: "You see, I let those whiskers grow for you, Grace." The little girl treasured the moment her whole life. She lived to be eighty-eight years old, dying in 1936.

AND TYLER TOO?

The president who turned his back on his country.

John Tyler is the only American president to commit a public act of treason against the United States government.

Tyler had been out of the White House for fifteen years when the Southern states began to secede, in 1860. A lifelong slave owner and states-rights advocate, he led an effort to find a compromise plan that could bring North and South together. He chaired a Peace Convention that convened in Washington in February of 1861. He avowed that his only goal was "to preserve the Government and to renew and invigorate the Constitution."

At the very same time, however, he was engaged in secret correspondence with Jefferson Davis, president of the Confederacy. When the Peace Convention's efforts failed, Tyler took up the Southern cause with gusto. He encouraged his native Virginia to join the other Southern states in rebellion. After it did, Tyler was elected to the Confederate Congress.

He died shortly thereafter, a member of a rebel government at war with the country he had once served as president.

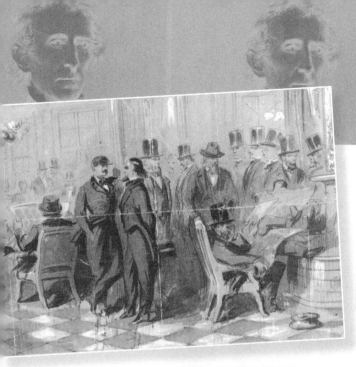

At the time of Tyler's death there were four other ex-presidents alive: Van Buren, Fillmore, Pierce, and Buchanan. All lived in the North and supported the Union to varying degrees.

e Peace Convention brought
gether 131 delegates from
enty-one states to the
llard Hotel in Washington.
ey represented a last-gasp
ort to avoid bloodshed.
t none of the states that
d already seceded from the
ion were represented, and
recommendations of the
ce Convention were rejected
Congress and incoming
sident Abraham Lincoln.

Photos of John Tyler taken as the Peace Convention met in Washington

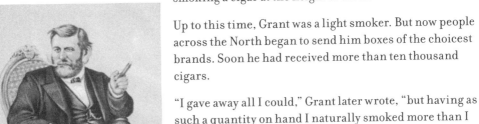

WHERE THERE'S SMOKE . . .

The general-turned-president who was a victim of his own fame.

In February of 1862, a little-known Union general named Ulysses S. Grant won a tremendous victory at Fort Donelson, Tennessee. After several days of sharp fighting, an entire Confederate army surrendered to Grant. He took more than twelve thousand prisoners.

Fort Donelson was the battle that made Grant famous. It was also the battle that killed him.

In the wake of the victory, Grant became the toast of the nation. Church bells in Northern cities rang out in celebration. Numerous articles were written about the victorious general. Several described him as smoking a cigar at the height of the battle.

Up to this time, Grant was a light smoker. But now people across the North began to send him boxes of the choicest brands. Soon he had received more than ten thousand cigars.

"I gave away all I could," Grant later wrote, "but having as such a quantity on hand I naturally smoked more than I would have done under the ordinary circumstances, and I have continued the habit ever since."

Grant, of course, went on to win the war and serve two terms as president. Twenty-three years after the battle, he died of throat cancer at age sixty-three. Doctors agreed that the cancer was brought on by his years of heavy cigar smoking. Fort Donelson had claimed its final victim.

This is the last photograph taken of
President Grant. He died a month
later, less than a week after finishing
his memoirs.

By the battle of the Wilderness, two years after Donelson, Grant
was secreting more than twenty cigars in his uniform pockets every
morning for smoking that day.

FAILED SPEECH

*Greatness is in the
ear of the beholder.*

Even the most successful public speaker comes up with a total flop once in a while. Take Abraham Lincoln, for example. Eloquent as he was, even Lincoln didn't always manage to enthrall all of the people all of the time.

There was one speech in particular that Lincoln knew in his heart had fallen short. The applause he received in response to his remarks was the first sign. It was barely enough to qualify as polite. Stepping down from the podium, he turned to an associate and delivered his judgment. "That speech won't scour. It is a flat failure."

Many in the press agreed. The *Chicago Times* reported, "The cheek of every American must tingle with shame as he reads the silly, flat, dish-watery utterances of . . . the President of the United States." A newspaper in Harrisburg, Pennsylvania, said simply, "We pass over the silly remarks of the president; for the credit of the nation we are willing that the veil of oblivion be dropped over them." The London *Times* told its readers, "Anything more dull and commonplace it would not be easy to produce."

What were the "silly remarks" made by the president that were nothing more than "dull and commonplace"? Ten sentences delivered in less than three minutes that have gone down in history as one of the greatest orations ever written in the English language:

The Gettysburg Address.

This is the only known picture to show Abraham Lincoln on the speakers' platform at Gettysburg. It was discovered in 1952 at the National Archives, and was most likely taken by Mathew Brady.

There were those at the time who saw the greatness of the speech. "The remarks of President Lincoln will live among the annals of man," reported the Chicago Tribune. The Springfield Republican called the speech "a perfect gem." Edward Everett, who spoke before Lincoln, said the president said more in two minutes than he did in two hours.

Executive Mansion,
Washington,   , 186 .

Four score and seven years ago our fathers brought forth, upon this continent, a new nation, conceived in liberty, and dedicated to the proposition that "all men are created equal."

Now we are engaged in a great civil war, testing whether that nation, or any nation so conceived and so dedicated, can long endure. We are met on a great battle field of that war. We have come to dedicate a portion of it, as a final resting place for those who died here that the nation might live. This we may, in all propriety do. But, in a larger sense, we can not dedicate—we can not consecrate—we can not hallow, this ground— The brave men, living and dead, who struggled here, have hallowed it, far above our poor power to add or detract. The world will little note, nor long remember...

WHAT DREAMS MAY COME

*The shocking
visions of a sleeping
president.*

Abraham Lincoln had many vivid dreams that he shared with his friends. In April of 1865, he told a few companions of a particularly powerful one from the night before.

Lincoln heard sobs, as if many people were weeping. In his dream, he left his bed and walked through the White House. The halls were empty, but he could still hear the same mournful sounds of distress.

I was puzzled and alarmed. What could be the meaning of all this? Determined to find the cause of a state of things so mysterious and so shocking, I kept on until I arrived at the East Room, which I entered.

There I met with a sickening surprise. Before me was a catafalque, on which rested a corpse wrapped in funeral vestments. Around it were stationed soldiers who were acting as guards; and there was a throng of people, gazing mournfully upon the corpse, whose face was covered, others weeping pitifully.

"Who is dead in the White House?" I demanded of one of the soldiers, "The President," was his answer; "he was killed by an assassin."

Three days later, Lincoln was shot by John Wilkes Booth. On Easter Sunday, he lay in state in the East Room, on a catafalque surrounded by soldiers.

Ward Lamon, a longtime Lincoln associate, was one of several people the president told about the dream. It was Lamon who wrote down and preserved Lincoln's description of it.

**ALTHOUGH IT WAS ONLY A
DREAM, I HAVE BEEN STRANGELY
ANNOYED BY IT EVER SINCE.** ❞

—ABRAHAM LINCOLN, THREE DAYS BEFORE HIS DEATH

*Lincoln presided over a cabinet meeting on the last day of his life. There he gave
Treasury Secretary Hugh McCulloch approval to form a new government agency to
fight counterfeiting. So it was that one of the last acts of the soon to be assassinated
president was to approve the establishment of the Secret Service. It would be
another thirty-six years before the service was formally given the job of protecting
presidents.*

THE MAN WHO SHOT BOOTH

The bizarre tale of Boston Corbett.

The forgotten man of Abraham Lincoln's assassination is the eccentric soldier who shot John Wilkes Booth. Born Thomas Corbett in England, he immigrated to Boston, where he became a reborn Christian. He adopted the city's name as his own in honor of his conversion.

Corbett's religious zeal knew no bounds. Fearing temptation by prostitutes, he used a pair of scissors to castrate himself, after which he casually attended a prayer meeting.

During the Civil War, Corbett became a cavalry sergeant. After the assassination, his unit took part in the search for Booth. On May 15, 1865, they surrounded the Virginia barn where Booth was hiding, and set it on fire. Corbett spotted Booth through a crack in the barn and fired a single shot into the assassin, mortally wounding him.

"Providence directed my hand," Corbett told his commanding officer.

Corbett became famous as "Lincoln's Avenger." He was deluged with requests for autographs and cheered when he walked down the street. Fame eventually slipped away, though, and Corbett began suffering from the delusion that Booth's friends were stalking him. He fled to Kansas.

In 1887 he was given as job as a doorkeeper to the Kansas House of Representatives. One day he showed up waving his gun, declaring the House adjourned. He was declared insane and sent to an asylum. The following year he escaped, and nobody ever heard of Boston Corbett again.

" WHAT A FEARFUL GOD WE SERVE. "

—CORBETT'S REACTION TO FINDING OUT THAT HIS BULLET HIT BOOTH IN THE SAME PLACE BOOTH'S BULLET HIT LINCOLN

Corbett was a hatter, and the mercury used to cure beaver pelts may have contributed to his madness.

Corbett received the same share of the reward money as every other member of his unit: $1,653.84.

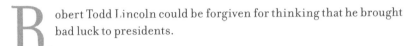

THE JINX

The twist of fate that linked one man with three assassinations.

Robert Todd Lincoln could be forgiven for thinking that he brought bad luck to presidents.

After President Abraham Lincoln was shot at Ford's Theatre, Robert was called to his father's side. He was there comforting his mother when his father died.

Fifteen years later, in 1881, Lincoln was secretary of war to President James Garfield. He came to the Washington train station to see Garfield off on a trip. Just as Lincoln arrived, a disgruntled office seeker gunned down the president. Lincoln was at Garfield's side within a few seconds of the shooting. The president was expected to recover, but eventually died from his wounds.

Some twenty years after that, in 1901, Lincoln was on his way to the Pan-American Exposition in Buffalo when he received news that President William McKinley had just been shot there. Lincoln rushed to the president's side later that day. McKinley was expected to recover, but died a week later.

Three presidents—and one man who might have had cause to wonder if he was the angel of death for each.

After Garfield was shot, Lincoln rushed to his side and sent his driver to get a doctor.

I n life, Robert Lincoln was connected with three presidential assassinations. In death he lies at Arlington Cemetery, just a few steps from the grave of the only other president to be gunned down by an assassin: John F. Kennedy.

THERE IS A CERTAIN FATALITY TO PRESIDENTIAL FUNCTIONS WHEN I AM PRESENT.

—A QUOTE ATTRIBUTED TO ROBERT TODD LINCOLN IN LATER YEARS

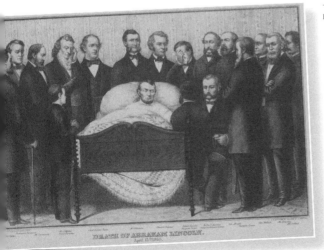

Robert Lincoln has a handkerchief to his face in this rendering of his father's deathbed.

THE MAN WHO SAVED THE PRESIDENCY

The Constitution saved, the presidency protected. By one vote.

The Senate chamber was hushed. All eyes were on Senator Edmund Ross of Kansas. "Hope and fear blended in every face," he recalled later. In Ross's hands lay the fate not only of the president but also of the presidency itself.

The scene was the impeachment trial of President Andrew Johnson, who had become president after the assassination of Abraham Lincoln. Radical Republicans who controlled Congress had come to hate Johnson, a Democrat, who they thought was being too easy on the South. The president vetoed bill after bill passed by Congress, and Republicans there determined to remove him from office. The House of Representatives impeached him on what were essentially trumped-up charges, and the Senate convened for trial.

At stake was the independence of the executive branch. If Congress could toss out any president it didn't like, the presidency itself might be weakened beyond repair. A vote count showed the Republicans just one shy of what they needed to convict. There was only one senator whose vote was in doubt.

Edmund Ross.

A Republican, Ross loathed Johnson and his policies. But he also believed the president deserved a fair trial, and shouldn't be removed for political reasons. As the only undecided vote, Ross was "hunted like a fox,"

according to the *New York Tribune*. Enormous pressure was put on him to convict. But he kept his own counsel until the final vote, on May 16, 1868.

"Mr. Ross, how say you?" intoned Chief Justice Salmon P. Chase.

"Not Guilty."

Republicans called Ross a "traitor," a "beast," a "skunk," and worse. Voters turned him out of office at the next election. He eventually became a Democrat and moved to New Mexico, where he was appointed territorial governor. Years later, even those who lambasted him at the time admitted that he had acted in the interest of the country. "By the firmness and courage of Senator Ross," said a Kansas newspaper that had once vilified him, "the country was saved from calamity greater than war."

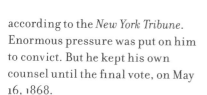

I ALMOST LITERALLY LOOKED DOWN INTO MY OPEN GRAVE.

—ROSS DESCRIBING THE MOMENT
WHEN HE HAD TO VOTE

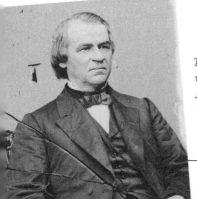

The charges against President Johnson were drawn up by his political enemies, who were looking for any reason they could to get rid of him. According to one of Johnson's cabinet members, if he had been accused of stepping on a dog's tail, that would have been enough to trigger an impeachment vote.

SPEED DEMON

"Mr. President, may I see your license, please?"

It was on a summer evening that the Washington, D.C., policeman saw the one-horse carriage careening down the street at high speed. The policeman, one of the capital's new black officers, flagged down the driver and berated him for zooming down the city street. It simply wasn't safe, he said. It was only when the policeman began writing out a citation that he realized just who the driver was.

President Ulysses S. Grant.

Grant fell in love with horses as a boy, and had a lifelong reputation as an exceptional horseman. When he became president he brought his favorite horses with him to the White House. In the evening he often went for a buggy ride to let off steam, and he liked to drive the buggies the way he had always liked to ride his horses—as fast as possible.

Upon recognizing Grant, the policeman tried to back off. But the president calmly told him that he was right in doing the job and to finish writing the ticket. The president paid the $20 fine on the spot. According to some accounts, his horse was impounded, and Grant had to walk home.

He remains the only president ever to receive a speeding ticket—a distinction he is unlikely to lose anytime soon.

Grant seemed to have a need for speed. In 1866, he was part of a presidential party traveling through New York City in two carriages, each led by a team of stunning horses. Grant took the reins of his carriage, and with a twinkle in his eye challenged the president's carriage to a race. In a flash the two carriages were flying through Central Park. Grant pulled ahead, and according to the New York Times, "the non-driving gentlemen of Mr. Grant's coach began to consider with some anxiety the probability of a safe arrival." Grant easily won the wild half-mile race. It is worth noting that one of the anxious gentlemen in his carriage was an impetuous cavalry officer named George Custer. He needn't have worried; his number wouldn't be called for another ten years.

Grant had a new barn built at the White House for his fast-stepping horses. One of them was a pony named Jeff Davis who bit everyone that came too close—except Grant.

THE BUFFALO HANGMAN

It's a dirty job, but somebody has to do it.

Numerous men who became president engaged in surprising occupations earlier in their careers. Theodore Roosevelt was a cowboy, Harry Truman was a haberdasher, and George W. Bush owned a baseball team. But no president has had a job quite like the one for which Grover Cleveland reluctantly volunteered.

He was an executioner.

Cleveland was elected sheriff of Erie County, New York, in 1870. The law called for the sheriff to handle all executions. A deputy named Jake Emerick had handled the job for many years, but he had officiated at so many hangings that he was becoming known as "Hangman Emerick," a source of great consternation to him and his family.

In 1872, Jack Morrissey was sentenced to die for executing his mother. The circumstances of the case generated a lot of sympathy for Morrissey, but he failed in his attempt to obtain a pardon. Cleveland announced that he would handle the execution himself, because he didn't feel he had the moral right to impose that burden on someone else.

On the appointed day, Sheriff Cleveland stood behind a screen some twenty feet from the gallows and pulled the lever that opened the trapdoor. Friends said he was sick at heart for days afterward. But in refusing to duck the ugly job, he started building a record of public integrity that would one day lead him to the White House.

Cleveland's opponents in the 1884 presidential election mocked him as "the Buffalo Hangman," but his supporters cited the incident as an example of his moral fiber.

Describing why he took the job, Cleveland said: "Jake and his family have as much right to enjoy public respect as I have, and I am not going to add to the weight that already brought him close to public execration." The following year he presided at a second execution for similar reasons.

MRS. SATAN

They called this devil-may-care presidential candidate "Mrs. Satan."

In May of 1872, the Equal Rights Party nominated Victoria Woodhull for president, before women even had the right to vote. She was a thirty-three-year-old social reformer who was also an outspoken advocate of free love. She told reporters it was a sure cure for immorality.

The flamboyant Woodhull took great delight in defying convention and breaking down barriers. A self-proclaimed clairvoyant who performed in her youth at carnivals, Woodhull and her sister achieved fame as America's first (and at that time, only) female stockbrokers, and published their own crusading newspaper.

When critics contended that Woodhull's promiscuity made her little better than a prostitute, she turned the tables: her paper accused one of the most famous ministers of the day, Henry Ward Beecher, of practicing sexual infidelity while preaching against it. Woodhull knew what she was talking about—she herself had been one of Beecher's lovers. The incendiary charges ignited a national sex scandal. Woodhull was jailed for pornography, and cartoonist Thomas Nast labeled her "Mrs. Satan."

The fact is, this extraordinary woman eventually married not the devil, but an English banker. The scandal stirred up so much hatred she fled the country. Leaving the tumult behind her, she created a new persona and lived out the second half of her life as a respected member of the British upper class.

Cornelius Vanderbilt fell under the spell of Woodhull and her sister, providing financial backing for their stock brokerage. The women played up to their reputation as spiritualists, claiming their stock picks came to them while in a trance. They made a fortune, and newspapers referred to them as "the Bewitching Brokers."

In 1871, Woodhull became the first woman to testify before Congress on the subject of women's suffrage. Later she met with President Grant, who she said gestured toward his desk and said, "Someday you will occupy that chair."

> " **MRS. WOODHULL, WITH AN AMBITION WORTHY OF A FEMALE NAPOLEON, GOES FOR THE PRESIDENCY.** "

—*NEW YORK TIMES*, MARCH 1870

Woodhull had only scorn for those who "preach against free love openly, and practice it secretly." She went after Beecher to illustrate what she considered to be a national double standard that gave men sexual freedom but denied it to women. Throughout the ensuing scandal, Beecher never denied her accusations.

BE SAVED BY FREE LOVE

THE BODY SNATCHERS

A grave threat to the president's security.

The plotters were determined to kidnap President Lincoln and hold him for ransom. It didn't seem to matter much to them that he had been dead for more than ten years.

The government had just put a master counterfeiter named Ben Boyd in prison. Members of the gang who pushed Boyd's phony bills were looking for a way to spring him. They came up with the bright idea of stealing Lincoln's body and holding it for ransom.

The gang planned to spirit Lincoln's body out of its tomb in Springfield, Illinois, on the one night nobody would notice: election night. After reburying the body in a carefully marked place, they would demand the government pay them $25,000 and release Boyd.

Things didn't quite work out the way they planned.

Somebody snitched on the snatchers, and the Secret Service infiltrated the gang. An agent and several Pinkerton detectives were waiting at the tomb the night of the heist. But they bungled things badly. The criminals got the body almost all the way out of the tomb before the detectives tried to apprehend them. In the gunfight that followed, the Pinkertons found themselves shooting at one another while the body snatchers got away.

Eventually two of the men were arrested, but they couldn't be charged with grave robbing for the simple reason that it wasn't a crime in Illinois! They were convicted instead of trying to steal the coffin, and served a year in jail.

The whole thing was enough to make the president roll over in his grave.

In the aftermath of the attempt, a band of Springfield citizens determined to protect the president's body secretly removed the president's coffin from the restored sarcophagus and hid it in a shallow grave between the walls of the memorial. It stayed there for decades.

Lincoln's tomb was rebuilt in 1900, and the president's body was reburied in a steel cage embedded in two tons of concrete, to ensure that no body snatchers would ever again be tempted to take it.

Grave robbing was a big problem in the late 1800s, with bodies being stolen for sale to medical schools. One body snatched in that manner was that of John Scott Harrison, who has the distinction of being the only man in American history whose father (William Henry Harrison) and son (Benjamin Harrison) were both elected president. Despite elaborate precautions, his body was stolen less than twenty-four hours after he was buried in 1878. It was found at the Ohio Medical School in Cincinnati, and eventually returned to its final resting place.

THE EDITOR AND THE ELECTION

The power of the press changes an election.

R epublican presidential candidate Rutherford B. Hayes went to bed on election night convinced that he had lost the election to Democrat Samuel Tilden. That's the story most of the nation's newspapers printed as well.

But *New York Times* managing editor John Reid wasn't convinced that Hayes had lost. He made sure that the headline in the *Times* reflected an election still in doubt. Then, being a dyed-in-the-wool Republican, he set out to do what he could to swing things for Hayes.

In the hours before dawn, Reid walked over to the Fifth Avenue Hotel, the headquarters of the Republican National Committee. He woke up party chairman Zachariah Chandler to argue that the election was not lost. "If you will only keep your heads there is no question of the election of President Hayes."

Chandler authorized editor Reid to do what he thought was needed. Reid promptly dictated telegrams to Republican leaders in Florida, Louisiana, South Carolina, and Oregon advising them that the election was still in doubt, and to fight for every vote. Reid rushed them to the telegraph office, and when the clerk told him that the Republicans didn't have an account, he charged the telegrams to the *Times*.

Reid's telegrams helped inspire Republicans to contest the results in those key battleground states. After months of bitter partisan wrangling that

Rutherford B. Hayes

divided the country, a special electoral commission voted along party lines to give the election to Hayes.

Thanks in part to the newspaper editor who wouldn't concede defeat.

THE PRESIDENTIAL ELECTION DEPENDS ON THE VOTE OF FLORIDA.

—REID TELEGRAM TO REPUBLICAN OPERATIVES IN FLORIDA.
IN AN EERIE REPLAY 124 YEARS LATER, THE BUSH-GORE ELECTION
ALSO CAME DOWN TO THE VOTES IN FLORIDA.

A special commission eventually voted on partisan lines to hand contested electoral votes in Florida and the other two states to the Republican Hayes. The House of Representatives did not officially declare Hayes president until just two days before the inauguration.

UNDERCOVER OATH

Only one president in history has taken the oath of office in secret.

The presidential election of 1876 was one of the closest and most disputed elections in history. The outcome was in dispute until a few days before the inauguration, when Republican Rutherford B. Hayes was declared the winner by one electoral vote.

Angry Democrats felt that the election had been stolen. Rumors were flying that they might try to do something about it. President Ulysses S. Grant ordered troops to Washington in case there was trouble.

Grant's term was due to expire at noon on Sunday, March 4. In observation of the Sabbath, Hayes's inauguration wasn't scheduled until Monday, March 5. Republicans feared that Democrats might somehow take advantage of the one-day gap to install Tilden in the White House or otherwise embarrass them.

They decided to take some preemptive action of their own.

Before a gala White House dinner on Saturday, March 3, Grant escorted Hayes to the Red Room. There, in front of a handful of cabinet members, Chief Justice Morrison Waite secretly administered the oath of office. The men returned to the dinner with no one else the wiser.

Hayes was publicly inaugurated the following Monday at noon, in front of a crowd of thousands who had no idea it was déjà vu all over again.

> ## I DID NOT ALTOGETHER APPROVE, BUT ACQUIESCED.

—RUTHERFORD B. HAYES, ON HIS EXTRAORDINARY SECRET OATH TAKING

Hayes took his secret oath in the Red Room. Democrats referred to him as "His Fraudulency." He served one term and didn't even try to run for re-election.

LET THE GOOD TIMES ROLL

A White House tradition created by a Congressional snit.

In the 1870s, the children of Washington, D.C., would turn the Capitol grounds into their own personal playground the Monday after every Easter. Families would set up picnics while children rolled decorated eggs around the grounds, egg rolling being a long-standing Washington custom.

In 1876, the assembled throngs left the Capitol grounds a mess. Congressmen, more comfortable with high rollers than egg rollers, promptly passed a law known as the Turf Protection Act. (Politicians, after all, love to protect their turf.) The new law sternly asserted that the Capitol grounds could no longer be used as a children's playground. As Easter of 1878 rolled around, Congress took out newspaper ads making it plain that Easter Monday egg rolling would not be tolerated at the Capitol.

What were the egg rollers to do?

A group of children approached President Rutherford B. Hayes while he was out on his daily constitutional. They begged him to let them use the White House lawn.

The president proved he wasn't as hardboiled as the eggheads on the other end of Pennsylvania Avenue. Hayes and his wife, Lucy, threw open the South Lawn of the White House to the egg rollers, and a new tradition was born. The White House Egg Roll has been a festive annual event ever since, except when weather, war, or White House renovations got in the way.

Leaving Congress with just a little bit of egg on its face.

A few hundred children and parents came that first year. By the 1930s, as many as fifty thousand were showing up for the White House egg roll. In recent years, due to security considerations, it has become a smaller, invitation-only event.

Every president since Hayes has attended at least one egg roll, including Bill Clinton, who got between the Easter Bunny and the camera in 1993.

ASSASSINATION TECH

The shooting of a president spurs the advance of technology.

In July of 1881, an unbalanced office seeker named Charles Guiteau shot President James Garfield in the back. Garfield was taken to the White House, where he lay in excruciating pain. Doctors feared he might die at any time. They searched in vain for the bullet so they could remove it.

That's when two of the country's most famous scientists got involved, with technologies that were years ahead of their time.

Dr. Alexander Graham Bell thought he had a way to find the bullet. He modified one of his telephones to create the world's first metal detector. When he passed a coil over metal, it made a hum that he could hear on the telephone receiver. Bell tested it on Civil War veterans who still carried around bullets in their bodies, and it worked every time. But when he tried it several times on the president, the results were inconclusive. Newspapers vilified him as a charlatan and a publicity seeker.

Meantime, navy engineers, led by astronomer Simon Newcomb, rigged up one of the world's first air conditioners to keep Garfield cool in Washington's searing heat. A container holding six tons of ice was set up in the basement. Air was blown over the ice, and then carried by a series of

Newcomb was a world-renowned astronomer and mathematician at the Naval Observatory in Washington. He calculated that cooling Garfield's room would require "a chest of ice nearly as long as an ordinary room, and large enough for men to walk about in." His cooling system consumed half a million pounds of ice over the two months it was used.

canvas ducts up to the president's room. It lowered the temperature there by more than twenty degrees.

The efforts of Bell and Newcomb helped move technology forward. But they weren't enough to save Garfield. He lingered on in great pain for eighty-one days before dying on September 19.

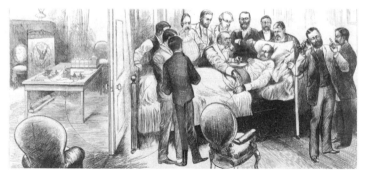

Bell called his metal detector an "induction balance." Why did it work on every patient he tried it on and then fail miserably with Garfield? Bell was unaware that Garfield was resting on a coil spring mattress—brand new at the time—and the coils foiled the metal detector. A later version enabled doctors in wartime to save numerous lives before the X-ray was invented.

The president might have survived if his doctors hadn't poked and prodded him with unwashed hands, infecting the president as they searched for the bullet. Guiteau used their incompetence as the centerpiece of his defense, saying he didn't kill Garfield: "The doctors did that. I simply shot at him." True as that might be, he was still convicted and hanged.

THIS OLD HOUSE

Surviving against the odds.

In 1814, an invading British army torched the White House. Only a thunderstorm prevented the building from burning to the ground. As it was, just the exterior walls were left standing. Some in Congress clamored to raze the ruins and move the capital city, but public sentiment, stirred up by the war, overruled the idea. The house was rebuilt.

In 1864, the commissioner of buildings pronounced the White House unfit for occupation. The occupant, Abraham Lincoln, kept on living there anyway.

Three years later, officials concerned about the dilapidated building drew up plans for a suburban White House, to be located on hundreds of acres outside the city. It would be a dazzling presidential palace, private and secure, isolated from the hubbub of downtown Washington. Then Grant became president. He and his wife, Julia, liked living in the old White House, right in the middle of things, and the plan fizzled.

In 1881, newly sworn-in president Chester A. Arthur was so horrified at the mansion's state of repair that he exclaimed: "I will not live in a house like this." Arthur proposed tearing the White House down and building a replica on the same spot. The Senate approved the idea, but the House never did.

Despite every effort, the "people's house" continued to stand, as it does today.

After failing to get a new house built, President Arthur spent more than $100,000 fixing up the existing building and having famed designer Louis Tiffany give the inside a makeover. As part of that effort, more than twenty-six wagonloads of furniture and other assorted items were auctioned off to the public.

The shell of the White House left by British invaders

By 1948 the White House was on the verge of falling apart. A piano broke through the second floor and landed in the dining room below. The building was completely gutted, but the exterior walls were left standing to preserve the legacy of the president's mansion.

VIEW·FROM·THE·SOUTH·
OF·THE·RESIDENCE·WINGS·
CONSERVATORY·AND·COURT·

First Lady Caroline Harrison proposed adding two enormous wings to the White House, which would have dramatically altered the look of the mansion. It goes without saying that this plan was never carried out.

THE PEABODY CONNECTION

The link between President Franklin Roosevelt and Wyatt Earp.

Wyatt Earp was a fixture of the Old West. Franklin Roosevelt gave us the New Deal. Wyatt was a pistol-packing marshal, while FDR tried to pack the Supreme Court. What possible connection could there be between them?

The answer lies with a man named Endicott Peabody.

Reverend Peabody was the founder and longtime headmaster of Groton Academy, a fabulously exclusive New England boarding school attended by the sons of wealthy Easterners. He was headmaster when Roosevelt attended the school, and became FDR's mentor. Roosevelt said Peabody had more influence on him than anyone but his parents. Reverend Peabody presided at the marriage of Franklin and Eleanor, and conducted prayer services before each of FDR's inaugurals.

But few realized that this scion of the Eastern establishment had some Wild West in his past.

In 1882, while studying for the ministry, Peabody spent six months doing missionary work in a wild and remote part of the world: Tombstone,

When Peabody arrived in Tombstone, the local paper took notice: "Well, we've got a parson who doesn't flirt with the girls, who doesn't drink beer behind the door, and when it comes to baseball, he's a daisy."

Arizona. Just a few months after the Earps and
Clantons shot it out at the OK Corral, Peabody was
helping to found Tombstone's first Episcopal church—
with some help from Earp's gambling winnings.

And so it was that two vastly different figures from
totally dissimilar periods in American history had
something in common: their spiritual adviser.

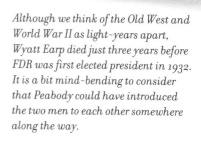

*Although we think of the Old West and
World War II as light-years apart,
Wyatt Earp died just three years before
FDR was first elected president in 1932.
It is a bit mind-bending to consider
that Peabody could have introduced
the two men to each other somewhere
along the way.*

*Peabody came to Tombstone's Oriental Saloon one day looking for funds to build his church. Earp forked over a stack of bills
from his winnings. "Here's my contribution, Mr. Peabody," he said. Then he told the other players they each needed to pony
up just as much. Peabody built the church, and Saint Paul's remains there to this day,*

AND THE TRUTH WILL SET YOU FREE

The cover-up that never happened.

When Democrat Grover Cleveland ran for president in 1884, he had a spotless reputation. The onetime mayor of Buffalo and governor of New York was known as honest and incorruptible. So squeaky clean was Cleveland that he was known as "Grover the Good."

Then came the news story that changed everything.

"A Terrible Tale," read the headline in the *Buffalo Evening Standard* just two weeks after Cleveland was nominated. The story reported that the bachelor candidate had a ten-year-old son born out of wedlock with a woman named Maria Halpin. The paper said he was secretly supporting his love child, named Oscar Cleveland.

This was a shocking scandal that threatened to sink Cleveland's candidacy. His campaign managers came to him in despair. What to do? Stonewall? Cover up? Spin? The marching orders that Cleveland gave them were radical in their simplicity.

"Whatever you say, tell the truth," he said. So they did.

The truth was that Cleveland had indeed had an affair with Maria Halpin. While he wasn't sure the child was his, he had done the honorable thing by assuming responsibility and offering child support.

The truth did the trick. Instead of tarnishing Cleveland, the affair only enhanced his honesty, and paved the way for his victory over Republican

James Blaine. The boy who may have been his illegitimate son grew up to be a doctor—under another name.

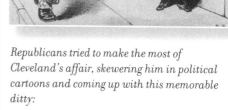

Cleveland's opponent, James Blaine of Maine, had to deal with scandals of his own. He had a reputation for slipperiness, and there was evidence suggesting that he had taken money while a congressman. Hence the Democrats' inspired chant:

*Blaine, Blaine,
James G. Blaine
Continental Liar from
the State of Maine!*

Republicans tried to make the most of Cleveland's affair, skewering him in political cartoons and coming up with this memorable ditty:

*Ma, Ma, where's my Pa?
Gone to the White House, ha ha ha!*

After Cleveland's victory, his supporters came up with the perfect response:

*Hurrah for Maria,
Hurrah for the kid,
We voted for Grover
And we're damn glad we did!*

CASTING A POLITICAL SPELL

Political speechmakers so effective it took a brand-new word to describe them.

The presidential election of 1888 pitted Democratic incumbent Grover Cleveland against Republican challenger Benjamin Harrison. From summer onward it was clear that this was going to be a very close election.

Republicans were determined to do everything possible to capture every possible vote. One arm of their operation that proved particularly successful was their speakers' bureau. A Kentucky politician named William Cassius Goodloe was the man in charge. He drafted the party's most popular orators and sent them on tours across the country. These silver-tongued luminaries set crowds on fire from coast to coast, and helped Harrison carry the day.

During the campaign, Goodloe coined a name for the most eloquent of Republican orators, inventing a word that that summed up their ability to hold audiences rapt with attention, as if a spell had been cast upon them.

He called them "the Spellbinders."

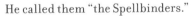

The word captured the public's fancy, and entered the popular lexicon. Today anytime we describe a book, or a movie, or a speech as "spellbinding" or a "spellbinder," we pay our respects, ever so briefly, to the long-forgotten political campaign in which the term originated.

After Cleveland's defeat, his wife told the White House staff to keep everything shipshape. "We'll be back in four years!" Her words proved prophetic. Cleveland defeated Harrison in 1892 and returned to the White House.

Almost exactly one year after the election, Cassius Goodloe's promising political career—and his life—came to an abrupt end in a Lexington, Kentucky, post office. There Goodloe ran into a longtime personal and political enemy named Amistead Swope. After the two exchanged words, Swope pulled out a pistol and shot Goodloe in the belly. The wounded Goodloe pulled out a pocketknife and began slashing at Swope, stabbing him more than a dozen times. Swope died within minutes, Goodloe a few days later. Former president Rutherford B. Hayes was one of the mourners at Goodloe's funeral.

Benjamin Harrison received a hundred thousand fewer votes than Cleveland but won in the electoral vote. It wasn't just because of the "Spellbinders." There was massive vote buying in at least two states, Indiana and New York. This prompted widespread outrage that led to adoption of the secret ballot, also known as the Australian ballot, which has been the hallmark of American elections ever since.

ANIMAL HOUSE

A glimpse of the other residents of the White House.

When First Lady Caroline Harrison moved into the White House in 1881, she was not pleased with her new home. It was cramped. It was shabby. Worse, it was infested.

With rats.

The First Lady came up with an innovative solution: she introduced an army of ferrets to the White House to combat the rat problem. But Mrs. Harrison was only one in a long line of people to introduce unusual animals to 1600 Pennsylvania Avenue.

One of the first was Marquis de Lafayette. When he came to visit in 1826, he brought along an alligator as a gift to President John Quincy Adams. The alligator lived for some months in a bathroom near the East Room. Martin Van Buren was given tiger cubs by the sultan of Oman and kept them for a while as pets.

Other out-of-the ordinary White House pets include Thomas Jefferson's grizzly cubs (a gift from Lewis and Clark), Dolley Madison's parrot, Louisa Adams's silkworms, William Howard Taft's pet cow, Pauline (left), and a whole menagerie of animals kept by Theodore Roosevelt's children, among them a wildcat, a hyena, and yes . . .

Snakes in the White House!

Rebecca the raccoon was a gift to President Coolidge from an admirer in Mississippi. She was intended to be the pièce de résistance at a Thanksgiving dinner. But Cal spared the raccoon, and his wife, Grace, adopted Rebecca as a pet. "She enjoyed nothing better," said Mrs. Coolidge, "than being placed in a bathtub with a little water in it and given a cake of soap with which to play. In this fashion she would amuse herself for hours."

The White House has also been the residence of numerous dogs, perhaps the most famous of which was FDRs Scotch terrier, Fala. When Republicans suggested during the 1944 campaign that the president had been wasting government money on Fala, Roosevelt gleefully fired back:

> These Republican leaders have not been content with attacks on me, or my wife, or on my sons. No, not content with that, they now include my little dog, Fala. Well, of course, I don't resent attacks. And my family doesn't resent attacks. But Fala does resent them!

SECRET SURGERY

One of the most successful White House cover-ups of all time.

In May of 1893, President Grover Cleveland noticed a rough spot on the roof of his mouth. His doctor found a cancerous growth the size of a quarter, and recommended immediate surgery.

Problem was, the country was going through some precarious financial times. More than two hundred banks had failed. White House aides feared that news of a presidential illness might send the economy into financial chaos. So the president, who had made candor his watchword—the man known as "Grover the Good"—launched a massive cover-up.

A team of five doctors secretly assembled on a private yacht in New York City. The main cabin was converted into a surgical suite. Cleveland came aboard the yacht the next day. The press was told he was headed on a pleasure cruise. But as soon as the boat began steaming up the river, the president was put under anesthesia and the operation began.

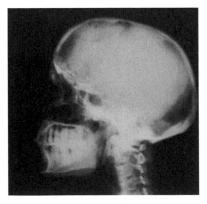

Doctors removed two teeth and most of Cleveland's upper left jaw. He was fitted with an artificial jaw made of vulcanized rubber. Special care was taken to avoid any scars that would be seen by the press. The yacht took the president to Cape Cod to recuperate. A spokesman told the press he was on vacation.

The operation was a success—the patient survived for another fifteen years. The cover-up was even more successful. The full story wasn't revealed until nearly forty years later.

When a Philadelphia newspaper reported that
Cleveland had undergone surgery on the yacht,
Secretary of War Daniel Lamont denied it. He told
reporters Cleveland had two teeth removed, and
was suffering from nothing more than "a bad
case of dentistry." The stonewalling effectively
killed the story.

The steam yacht Oneida, aboard which the surgery took place

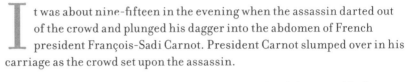

THE CUTTING EDGE

*The presidential
assassination that
inspired a medical
breakthrough.*

It was about nine-fifteen in the evening when the assassin darted out of the crowd and plunged his dagger into the abdomen of French president François-Sadi Carnot. President Carnot slumped over in his carriage as the crowd set upon the assassin.

The dagger severed an artery leading to the president's liver, and he began to bleed profusely. The best surgeons in Paris were summoned, but they could do nothing. President Carnot died with hours.

A young medical student in Lyons was struck by the fact that if doctors had known how to repair the artery, it might have saved the president's life. Alexis Carrel promptly began to search for a way to do it. The son of a silk manufacturer, he sought out one of the leading silk embroiderers in Lyons, Madame Leroudier, to tutor him in the use of tiny needles and fine thread. His efforts turned him into one of the finest surgeons in France. He also developed innovative techniques to avoid clotting and fight off infection.

Within five years he had successfully developed a technique to sew severed blood vessels back together.

Carrel's work won him the 1912 Nobel Prize. More than that, it became the foundation for all organ transplant work, first pioneered by him and later by others. President Carnot could not know that the lives of many would be saved by his own unfortunate death.

President François Carnot was stabbed by an Italian anarchist named Cesare Santo. He had been president of France for nearly seven years at the time of his death.

Carrel later collaborated with Charles Lindbergh to invent a pump designed to circulate blood during a transplant procedure.

FIFTEEN CENTS

TIME
The Weekly Newsmagazine

Volume XXXI

Painted for TIME by S. J. Woolf

LINDBERGH, CARREL & PUMP
They are looking for the fountain of age.
(see MEDICINE)

Number 24

LABOR DAY

The irony behind the holiday.

President Grover Cleveland signed a law making Labor Day a national holiday. In creating a holiday honoring workers, he handed organized labor a huge victory. President Cleveland also sent soldiers to battle striking workers in Chicago. In using the army to violently crush the strike, he handed organized labor a stunning defeat.

Now for the amazing part: he did both those things within four days of each other.

In May of 1894, workers at the Pullman Palace Car Company in Chicago went on strike after receiving a 25 percent pay cut. When the company refused to submit to arbitration, fifty thousand railroad workers across the country refused to work on any train with a Pullman car. Rail traffic was slowed to a crawl, and violence was in the air.

By June 28, one newspaper reported that the strike had "assumed the proportions of the greatest battle between labor and capital that has ever been waged in the United States." That very same day, President Grover Cleveland signed into law a bill making the first Monday of every September a national holiday: Labor Day.

The timing may seem odd, but the bill was probably intended to calm labor unrest. What the president did four days later was not.

The leader of the American Railway Union, Eugene V. Debs, was jailed for six months for his role in the Pullman strike. Debs read Karl Marx in jail and became a socialist. He ran for president six times on the Socialist Party ticket. Debs was jailed again in 1920, this time for making an antiwar speech during World War I. Running from his cell, he polled nearly a million votes.

In response to reports of violence, Cleveland declared that the strikers were disrupting the U.S. mail, and sent soldiers to establish martial law. Within days, soldiers and strikers clashed, and seven men were killed. Union leaders were jailed and the strike was brutally put down. The action crippled the labor movement in America for decades.

Yet the holiday endured.

A union leader named Peter McGuire was the first to propose the idea of a holiday to celebrate workers, back in 1882. Twenty-three states adopted it as a holiday before President Cleveland made it into a national holiday in 1894.

" IF IT TAKES THE
ENTIRE ARMY AND
NAVY OF THE UNITED
STATES TO DELIVER
A POSTCARD IN
CHICAGO, THAT CARD
WILL BE DELIVERED. "

—PRESIDENT GROVER CLEVELAND

BUTTONED UP

*Pinning your hopes
right on your lapel.*

Amanda Lougee didn't set out to forever change presidential campaigns. But the Boston woman nevertheless helped do just that.

Lougee was something of a rarity for her time—a female entrepreneur. She took over a small rubber factory on the death of her brother and built it up into a nationally known company that employed nearly three hundred people, making everything from clothing to electrical tape. In her spare time she was an avid supporter of the suffragette movement, even contributing a fruitcake recipe to *The Woman's Suffrage Cookbook.*

She was also a bit of an inventor. In 1893, she filed a patent for a new way of making a button covered with material. A New Jersey printing company called Whitehead and Hoag saw a use for her idea that she never anticipated. They snapped up her patent and two others, and in 1896 came out with something brand new.

The modern campaign button.

The buttons were cheap to make, and soon became all the rage. It has been said that no innovation in politics ever gained acceptance faster. More than a thousand different kinds of buttons were made for the 1896 presidential campaign pitting William McKinley against William Jennings Bryan. And they've been a staple of every campaign since.

In the original buttons, one side of a metal disk was covered with a piece of paper, and that in turn was covered with clear celluloid. Starting in 1916, the images began to be printed directly on the metal.

Collectors have paid as much as $50,000 for certain rare campaign buttons. One of the rarest is a button showing 1920 Democratic candidate James Cox and his running mate, Franklin D. Roosevelt.

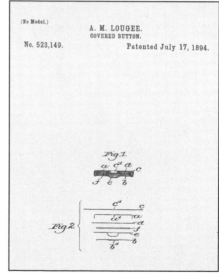

(No Model.)

A. M. LOUGEE.
COVERED BUTTON.

No. 523,149.   Patented July 17, 1894.

Fig. 1.

Fig. 2

THE PRESIDENT AND THE PRIEST

How procrastination led to an assassination.

On October 28, 1893, Chicagoans were shocked to learn that an assassin had shot to death their mayor, Carter Harrison. One of those deeply affected by the shooting was a Polish priest named Casimir Zeglen. He became consumed with the idea of designing a practical bulletproof material that might save innocent lives in the future.

Four years later, Father Zeglen succeeded in coming up with the world's first truly practical bulletproof vest—light enough to wear under clothing, but strong enough to stop a bullet. It consisted of wafer-thin steel plating sandwiched inside layers of tightly woven silk.

He first tested it on a cadaver, then on a Great Dane, and finally, in several dramatic public demonstrations, on himself. It worked perfectly every time.

Zeglen left the priesthood to found the Zeglen Bullet Proof Cloth Company. As part of his promotional efforts, he contacted the White House in 1901 to offer President William McKinley a vest. The president's personal secretary expressed a genuine interest but said the matter couldn't be considered until after the president's trip to the Pan-American Exposition in Buffalo, New York.

He shouldn't have waited.

It was in Buffalo that assassin Leon Czolgosz walked up to McKinley and shot him twice at point-blank range. Had the president been wearing the

HE FEARS NOT BULLETS

Father Zeglen Acts as a Target in a Successful Test of His Own Armor Cloth.

POLISH PRIEST'S INVENTION

Exhibition of a Shot-Proof Fabric That Is Designed to be Worn with Ordinary Attire—Military Test Asked For.

The Rev. Father Casimir Zeglen of the Redemptionist Brotherhood, in Chicago, has invented a bullet-proof cloth, in which he has so much confidence that he stands as a target for bullets with only a small piece of his armor-fabric as a shield.

An informal exhibition of Father Zeglen's invention was witnessed by several military men, Consuls of foreign nations, and newspaper men on the stage of Koster & Bial's Music Hall yesterday afternoon.

The inventor was introduced by Dr. Gustave H. Morré of the United States Immigration Service, who explained that Father Zeglen was a native of Poland, and did not speak the English language very well.

Dr. Morré said the assassination of Carter Harrison in Chicago four years ago suggested to Father Zeglen the idea of a bullet-proof cloth that could be worn in ordinary every-day attire by men of

Exhibition of a Shot-Proof Fabric
That Is Designed to be Worn
with Ordinary Attire

vest, he would have lived and Zeglen would have become famous. Instead, McKinley died eight days later, and Theodore Roosevelt became president. Zeglen never achieved the level of success he sought. And history was left with an intriguing "What if?"

Zeglen tried and discarded all sorts of material for his vest: steel shavings, moss, hair, and others. Finally he hit on silk. He consulted with Polish weavers in Vienna to achieve the perfect weave required to dissipate the energy of the bullet.

Archduke Ferdinand was wearing a Zeglen vest when an assassin in Sarajevo shot him in 1914. Unfortunately, Gavrilo Princip aimed high, hitting the archduke in the neck, where the vest didn't protect him. The assassination led to the start of World War I.

GUESS WHO'S COMING TO DINNER?

A groundbreaking meal at the White House.

One month after he became president, Theodore Roosevelt invited a prominent educator to dinner at the White House. The two men had a quiet meal with Roosevelt's wife, Edith, and a family friend.

The result was a national controversy.

Roosevelt's guest was Booker T. Washington, the head of Tuskegee University and the first African American to be invited to dine at the White House.

Reaction from the South was explosive. "White men of the South, how do you like it?" shouted the *New Orleans Times Democrat*. "White women of the South, how do YOU like it?" Headlines in many other Southern papers were just as angry. "A Damnable Outrage," said the *Memphis Scimitar*. "Roosevelt Dines a Darkey," said the *Richmond Dispatch*.

Southern politicians were also quick to condemn Roosevelt. "No self-respecting Southern man can ally himself with the President after what has occurred," thundered the governor of Georgia. Hate mail and death threats poured into the White House.

The intensity of the response surprised Roosevelt. "No one could possibly be as astonished as I was," he wrote a friend. Publicly he declared that he wouldn't back down to those

criticizing his dinner with Washington. "I shall have him to dine just as often as I please." Nevertheless, while Roosevelt continued to consult Washington, and met with him again at the White House, he never again had him to dinner.

SOCIAL EQUALITY WITH THE NEGRO MEANS DECADENCE AND DAMNATION.

—SOUTH CAROLINA LIEUTENANT GOVERNOR
JAMES TILLMAN, CONDEMNING THE DINNER

Not all of the reaction was negative. A number of Northern newspapers praised Roosevelt, and many African Americans expressed their appreciation. "Greatest step for the race in a generation," telegraphed a black man from Nashville.

EQUALITY

TEDDY BEAR

How a president's compassion inspired America's favorite toy.

President Theodore Roosevelt was an avid outdoorsman. In 1902, on a trip to Mississippi, he was invited on a hunting trip.

Hunting dogs ranging far ahead cornered a bear in a lagoon. The men bringing up the lead in the hunting party wanted to save the kill for the president, so they roped the bear to a tree.

But when TR arrived, he refused to shoot the now helpless animal.

The *Washington Star* ran a cartoon by Clifford Berryman showing Roosevelt refusing to shoot a cowering bear cub. The cartoon struck a chord in the mind of a Brooklyn toy store owner named Morris Mitchom. He asked his wife, Rose, to help create a stuffed bear, which he displayed in his storefront window alongside a picture of Teddy Roosevelt.

Mitchom even wrote to the president asking if he could use his name to promote the new bear. Back came a letter from the White House. "I don't think my name is likely to be worth much in the bear business, but you're welcome to use it."

The president was wrong about the value of his name. Mitchom was right about his new toy, and the "Teddy Bear" quickly became a national sensation.

Public response was so great to this cartoon that Berryman began putting little bear cubs into many other cartoons of the president.

DRAWING
THE LINE
IN MISSISSIPPI

Contrary to legend, Roosevelt did not spare the life of the bear tied to the tree. He simply refused to shoot it himself. One of the other hunters killed the bear with a knife, drenching himself with blood in the process.

The first Teddy Bear was about two and a half feet tall, and covered with honey-colored plush.

SPELLBOUND

How do you spell
"bad move"?

Teddy Roosevelt was a poor speller since childhood. As president, he became an enthusiastic supporter of efforts to simplify the spelling of English words. In 1906, he ordered that all White House documents be printed with revised spellings of three hundred words proposed by spelling reformers. "Through" would be spelled "thru" and "dropped" would be spelled "dropt," for example.

It may have been the biggest miscalculation of his career.

An international uproar ensued. Congressmen made impassioned speeches, accusing the activist president of going too far. Editorial writers had a field day. The *Baltimore Sun* asked whether TR's name should now be spelled "Rusevelt" or "Butt-in-sky."

British newspapers responded with outrage and mockery. "How dares this Roosevelt fellow," fumed the *London Evening Standard,* "presume to dictate to us how to spell a language which was ours while America was still a savage and undiscovered country?" Said the *London Sun*: "We ventur to think that even Prezident Ruzvelt mite manage to get along very wel with the langwige that was gud enuf for Shakespeare and Milton."

Roosevelt's enemies seized the opportunity to gang up on him. After the House voted 142-24 to overturn TR's order, the president reluctantly backed off. His efforts to change the way Americans spell?

Thru.

Efforts to reform the spelling of American English predate the Declaration of Independence. Benjamin Franklin championed the idea of revising the alphabet itself, removing six consonants and replacing them with four new consonants and two new vowels.

E veryone had something to say on the controversy. One person at the U.S. Pension Office with way too much time on his hands reported that he had counted 1,690 different spellings of the word "diarrhea" in pension applications.

THE MAN WHO SAVED FOOTBALL

Another thing we owe to President Roosevelt: the forward pass.

In October of 1905, President Theodore Roosevelt convened an urgent summit meeting at the White House. The subject: college football. The game had become so brutal that more than a hundred student players had died. College presidents were disbanding teams. Several state legislatures were giving serious consideration to making football illegal.

TR liked football (his son played football at Harvard), but he had a harsh message for the men who ruled the game: change football to make it safer, or the rising public outcry might force him to ban it.

Roosevelt's call for reform prompted the formation of a new rules committee to make major changes to the game. One committee member suggested an idea long advocated by legendary coach John Heisman: legalizing the forward pass. That might open up the game, reducing dangerous mass collisions in the middle of the field.

The *New York Times* called the idea "radical," and the head of the rules committee was opposed to it. Nevertheless it was adopted for the 1906 season, along with other rules that outlawed holding and unnecessary roughness, and required a team to gain ten yards (instead of five) for a first down.

Though football purists decried the changes, they wound up making the game not only safer but also more popular than ever. Football passed into a new era, thanks to a play called by the president.

The New Game of FOOTBALL

Radical changes ••• •• in this year's rules revolutionize the sport

The new rules legalized the forward pass but heavily restricted its use. The ball could not be passed within five yards of the center, it could not be passed to a receiver in the end zone, and an incomplete pass automatically resulted in the other team getting the ball.

College football's first forward pass came on September 22, 1906, when Saint Louis University quarterback Brad Robinson heaved the ball to Jack Schneider in a game against Carroll College. (Robinson later became mayor of Saint Louis.) Saint Louis coach Eddie Cochems, an unsung pioneer of the passing game, was among the first to teach his players to throw the ball with their fingers on the laces to get a good spiral.

> ## GET THE GAME PLAYED ON A THOROUGHLY CLEAN BASIS!

—PRESIDENT THEODORE ROOSEVELT TO
COLLEGE FOOTBALL OFFICIALS

COURT OF APPEAL

The case of the man who didn't want to be president.

All his life, William Howard Taft had one great ambition: he wanted to be chief justice of the United States. President Theodore Roosevelt thought Taft would be a great Supreme Court justice and wanted to appoint him to the court. But one person stood in his way.

Taft's wife.

When Nellie Taft was seventeen, she confided to her girlfriends that her goal in life was to marry a man who would become president. She didn't want her husband on the court. She wanted him in the White House. And she was determined to get her way,

In 1906, TR offered Taft the next opening on the court. Taft wanted to accept. His wife told him he would be making the biggest mistake of his life. It led to a West Wing showdown between Nellie Taft and Theodore Roosevelt. There is no record of the conversation that took place between these two strong-willed people. But according to White House chief usher Ike Hoover, "It was only through the pleadings of Mrs. Taft that he was not appointed [to the court]."

Nellie Taft had her lifelong wish fulfilled. Her husband was elected president. But Taft got his way too. After being defeated in a halfhearted bid for reelection, he was appointed chief justice by President Woodrow Wilson, becoming the only man to serve in both positions.

One night at a White House dinner, TR teased the Tafts by saying he saw a silver string above Taft's head. He said he couldn't tell if it said "President" or "Chief Justice." "Make it the presidency," said Nellie. "Make it the chief justiceship," said Taft.

As First Lady, Nellie Taft helped transform a muddy patch of land alongside the Potomac into a park with a grandstand. She suggested lining the road to the park with Japanese cherry blossom trees. The Japanese government offered the trees as a gift, and she planted the first one in 1912. Within a few years the cherry blossom trees had became one of Washington's most distinctive tourist attractions.

As president, the 330-pound Taft got stuck more than once in the White House bathtub, and had to be pulled out. So a new tub was installed—one that was seven feet long and nearly four feet wide, and could fit four more-normal-sized men.

PRESIDENTIAL PHRASEMAKER

One president who truly had a way with words.

Theodore Roosevelt was more than an activist president. He was perhaps the greatest phrasemaker to ever inhabit the White House. His contributions to the English language still affect the way we talk.

It was Roosevelt who first called the White House "a bully pulpit," a great stage for someone to use to make his views heard round the world. He is also famous for the proverb "Speak softly and carry a big stick."

It didn't stop there. TR also came up with "lunatic fringe" to refer to the extremists that populate all political parties. Asked in 1912 whether he would run for president again, the president introduced yet another enduring phrase. This one referred to frontier boxing, when a man ready to take on all challengers would toss his hat into the boxing ring.

"My hat's in the ring."

Roosevelt has also been credited with accidentally authoring one of the enduring marketing slogans of the twentieth century. In 1907, Roosevelt visited the Hermitage, the Tennessee home of President Andrew Jackson. Given a cup of coffee, he drank it down it and then supposedly exclaimed:

"Delighted! Good to the last drop!"

The coffee was a local brew served at the Maxwell House, one of Nashville's hotels. Within a decade, Maxwell House coffee began using the slogan to turn the coffee into a powerhouse national brand.

TR had struck again.

The original Maxwell House burned down in 1961.

There's some disagreement over whether Roosevelt actually uttered, "Good to the last drop" during his visit to the Hermitage, although at least one eyewitness said he did. There is no doubt that he raved over the coffee he was served. A local paper captured this quote: "This is the kind of stuff I like to drink, by George, when I hunt bears."

THE SHAPE OF THE PRESIDENCY

From Washington to Watergate, the story of the Oval Office.

I t's the most famous room in the White House. Perhaps in the world. Decisions made in the Oval Office impact everyone on the globe. But how did the president's office come to be an oval, and when did we start referring to it that way?

It all has to do with how George Washington liked to greet people.

Upon becoming president, George Washington moved into a house in Philadelphia, then serving as the nation's capital. Washington liked to hold formal receptions where guests gathered in a circle to meet him. He replaced the square corners of two rooms in the house with semicircular walls to make them more suitable for these "levees." When James Hoban designed the White House, he catered to Washington's desires by including an oval drawing room, the Blue Room.

More than a century later, in 1909, when architect Nathan Wyeth was designing a new West Wing office for the president, he wanted to give it a "dignified treatment" in keeping with its high purpose. In tribute to the Blue Room, and Washington, he created an oval office. But the term "Oval Office" was not widely used . . . at least not for sixty years.

During the Watergate scandal, aides to President Nixon started using the phrase "Oval Office" to talk about the involvement of the president without actually using his name. The phrase exploded into public usage, and has been with us ever since.

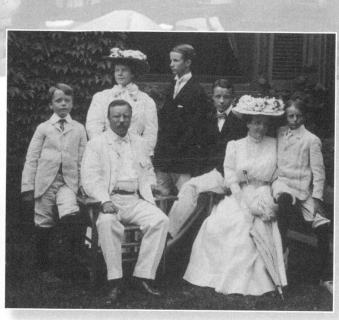

The West Wing was added to the White House in 1902, in large part because Theodore Roosevelt's large and rambunctious family was making the building too crowded. It was supposed to be temporary, but it is still there.

In 1909, President Taft, the largest of the presidents, supervised the enlargement of the West Wing, adding the Oval Office. Some have jokingly suggested its shape reflects his rotund body.

President Franklin Roosevelt enlarged the West Wing again in 1934, to accommodate burgeoning staff. He had the Oval Office moved to its current site, on the southeast corner of the building.

YOU'RE OUT!

Baseball could have cost Dwight D. Eisenhower the White House.

Dwight Eisenhower is the only president ever to play professional baseball. He played a couple of seasons on a minor league team in the Kansas State League. He apparently played one summer before he attended West Point, and another summer between his first and second years at the military academy. "I went into baseball deliberately to make money," he said later, "with no idea of it being a career."

Ike played center field, but you won't find his name in any league records or newspaper accounts of its games. That's because he played under an assumed name: Wilson. You might say that he was engaged in his first cover-up more than forty years before entering the White House. He took the alias because he knew that playing even a handful of games could disqualify him from college athletics, given the strict amateur code of the time.

His deception could have had far more grave consequences.

As a West Point student athlete, Eisenhower had to pledge that he had never played professional sports. Lying on that pledge was a violation of the West Point honor code. If anyone had found out, Eisenhower's military career and his storied rise to president might never have happened.

Eisenhower is fourth from left in this picture of his high school baseball team.

> 66 I TOLD HIM I WANTED TO BE A REAL MAJOR LEAGUE BASEBALL PLAYER. . . . MY FRIEND SAID THAT HE'D LIKE TO BE PRESIDENT OF THE UNITED STATES. NEITHER OF US GOT OUR WISH. 99

—DWIGHT D. EISENHOWER, RECOUNTING A CONVERSATION WITH A FRIEND THAT HE HAD AS A SMALL BOY

Eisenhower remained guarded about his baseball past. He first revealed it in a conversation with New York Giants manager Mel Ott in 1945, but offered few details. When Ott asked him what position he played, Eisenhower said, "That's my secret." Later he instructed his staff not to answer questions about his professional baseball days because it could get "too complicated."

Like Eisenhower, legendary athlete Jim Thorpe played minor league baseball while still an amateur. It cost him his Olympic gold medals, although they were reinstated after his death. Eisenhower and Thorpe had something else in common: they played football against each other on November 9, 1912. Thorpe's Carlisle College decimated West Point 27-6. When Ike and a teammate tried to tackle the dazzling Thorpe late in the second half, the two cadets ran into each other and were so stunned they had to be removed from the game. Eisenhower injured his knee in a game against Tufts the following week, and his athletic career was over.

FIRST IN THE NATION

How frugality gave birth to a presidential rite of passage.

It all began in 1906, when Winston Churchill decided he wanted to run for governor of New Hampshire. No, not *that* Winston Churchill. This Winston was a popular American writer of the same name.

When he sought the Republican nomination for governor, however, he was defeated at a rigged convention. The resulting outrage eventually led reformers to establish New Hampshire's first political primary. Initially it was just for state offices. Then, in 1913, the presidential race was added.

The state's first presidential primary was scheduled for May of 1916. But someone suggested that it would be cheaper to hold the primary on the same day all the towns in New Hampshire held their annual town meetings: the second Tuesday in March. Granite Staters pride themselves on their frugality, and the date was changed. So it came to be that New Hampshire had the first presidential primary in the country.

At first nobody cared. The voting was only for delegates, and most of them ran as uncommitted. Interest and turnout were so low that in 1949 the legislature added a "beauty contest," where people could also vote for which presidential candidate they preferred.

This caught the nation's eye.

In 1952, the "first in the nation" primary gave an important boost to the candidacy of General Dwight Eisenhower and abruptly ended the third-term hopes of incumbent Harry Truman. It has never left the political spotlight since.

New Hampshire is one of the smallest states in the Union, but its primary has made and broken many candidacies since 1952, while offering more than its share of media moments.

In 1968, President Lyndon Johnson dropped out of the race after challenger Eugene McCarthy came from nowhere to garner a better-than-expected 42 percent of the Democratic vote.

In 1972, Democratic front-runner Senator Ed Muskie choked up while responding to personal attacks by the Manchester Union Leader. The Muskie crying incident, as it came to be called, suggested that he couldn't handle the pressures of the campaign, and proved devastating to his candidacy.

In 1976, a win in the New Hampshire primary helped catapult a little-known Southern governor named Jimmy Carter to front-runner status.

After a disastrous showing in the Iowa caucuses, Vice President Bush rebounded to defeat Senator Bob Dole in the 1988 New Hampshire primary, going on to win the nomination and the election.

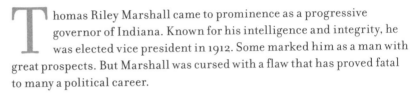

A NICKEL FOR YOUR THOUGHTS

The vice president who managed to achieve five cents' worth of fame.

Thomas Riley Marshall came to prominence as a progressive governor of Indiana. Known for his intelligence and integrity, he was elected vice president in 1912. Some marked him as a man with great prospects. But Marshall was cursed with a flaw that has proved fatal to many a political career.

He had a keen sense of humor. And he wasn't shy about using it.

As a result he came to be viewed by some contemporaries as a bit of a lightweight. But it is because of his sense of humor that we remember him at all today.

As vice president, Marshall presided over the Senate. One day Senator Joseph Bristow of Kansas was making a long and tedious speech about what was the matter with the country, and how to fix it. Paragraph after paragraph began with the phrase "What this country needs is . . . ," and according to Bristow, the country needed a lot.

Finally the VP had had enough. As Bristow droned on, Marshall leaned down to Senate clerk Henry Rose and spoke to him in a stage whisper that everyone could hear.

Marshall was famous for his humorous asides. Late in life, his career in politics over, he published a compilation of them. He wrote it, as he said, "in the hope that the tired businessman, the unsuccessful golfer and the lonely husband whose wife is out reforming the world may find therein a half hour's surcease from sorrow."

"Henry," he said, "what this country really needs is a good five-cent cigar."

Marshall's remark punctured Bristow's pomposity and captured the nation's fancy. The vice president was deluged with boxes of cigars from people across the country, and his remark was remembered long after his name faded.

What is it with presidents and cigars? In 1962, John F. Kennedy sent Press Secretary Pierre Salinger out on a mission one night to round up thousands of his favorite brand of Cuban cigar. The bewildered Salinger reported to the president the next morning that he had done so. "Thank goodness," said Kennedy. "I can sign this." He then put his signature on a trade embargo with Cuba that banned, among other things, the import of Cuban cigars.

At the time of Marshall's remark, most first-class cigars cost a dime.

WARTIME WOOL

Putting the presidency out to pasture.

As U.S. forces headed "over there" during World War I, President Woodrow Wilson and his wife looked for visible ways to demonstrate their support for the troops. One of the ideas they decided to put into effect:

Sheep on the White House lawn.

The Wilsons brought in a flock of prize sheep to graze on the grounds at the White House. The idea was that the sheep would save the manpower required to cut the grass, and that their wool could be auctioned off to supply money for the Red Cross.

The sheep took up residence outside the White House in April of 1918. Among them was a ram named Old Ike that liked to chew tobacco. After the sheep were sheared, two pounds of wool was sent to each state to be put up for auction. The wool that went to Massachusetts sold for $1,000 a pound in an auction held on Boston Common, making it the most expensive wool of all time.

The herd grazed on the grounds of the White House for two years before being shipped back to the Maryland farm they came from.

White House wool auctioned off in 1918 netted more than $50,000 for the Red Cross.

ANALYZE THIS

Did a personality disorder get in the way of a president's peace plans?

Woodrow Wilson was the only U.S. president to be psychoanalyzed by Sigmund Freud. Of course, the famous Austrian neurologist never actually got Wilson on the couch. But he was so fascinated by Wilson that he coauthored a book applying the tools of psychoanalysis to the president.

Wilson was already dead, but Freud considered his analysis to be so controversial that he didn't want it made public until Wilson's wife had also passed away. The book wasn't published until 1966, more than twenty-five years after Freud's own death.

Freud and coauthor William Bullitt, who had worked as an adviser to Wilson, diagnosed the president as suffering from severe personality defects that prevented him from achieving a lasting peace after World War I. (Wilson failed in his efforts to get the U.S. Senate to ratify the Versailles Peace Treaty or enter the League of Nations, largely due to his own intransigence.) Freud saw in Wilson a neurotic who was dominated by his father, overprotected by his mother, and who lacked the masculine will to carry out his policies. Freud also thought Wilson suffered from a savior complex and needed to be worshipped to satisfy the demands of his superego.

The book was one of the first that sought to psychoanalyze a public figure, and critics assailed it. Freud wouldn't have been surprised. "What progress we are making," he once said. "In the Middle Ages they would have burned me. Now they are content with burning my books."

Woodrow Wilson and Sigmund Freud were both born in the same year, 1856.

Freud (left) wrote the book with William Bullitt (right). Bullitt later served as ambassador to Russia and secretary of the navy. Some critics suggested that Bullitt held a long-standing grudge against Wilson, and used Freud to help score points against the late president.

Freud described Wilson's most trusted adviser, Colonel Edward House, as the president's "chief love object."

CONVOY

The road trip that changed America.

In the summer of 1919, the U.S. Army organized a coast-to-coast expedition of military vehicles to show off its equipment and demonstrate the need for better roads.

More than half of the trip was over dirt roads that were little better than trails. Broken-down bridges had to be repaired along the way, and soldiers frequently had to get out to dig trucks out of the mud or push them through difficult sections. In the end, it took the eighty-one vehicles of the Transcontinental Motor Convoy a grueling sixty-two days to cross the country.

The journey was to have a major impact on the American landscape.

One young army officer accompanied the mission "partly as a lark, and partly to learn." His name was Dwight Eisenhower, and the long, hard trip convinced him that better roads were an important national priority. That conviction was strengthened by his experience as supreme allied commander in Europe. "The old convoy had started me thinking about good two-lane highways, but Germany had made me see the wisdom of broader ribbons across the land."

And so it was that thirty-five years after the convoy struggled across the nation, President Eisenhower took up the cause of a modern interstate highway system. His efforts resulted in the construction of more than forty thousand miles of interstate highways. Small signs along those highways mark them as part of the Eisenhower Interstate System—and now you know the story behind that.

"We were not sure if it could be accomplished at all," said Eisenhower of the expedition. "Nothing of the sort had ever been attempted."

Wyoming.

Hoping it will hold.

Lemonade — gratis.

Scenes from the rugged western portions of the journey. Eisenhower made the handwritten captions. The convoy passed through 350 communities in eleven states, and was witnessed by an estimated 3 million people.

THE WOMAN WHO BECAME PRESIDENT

She may not have had the title, but she was certainly woman enough for the job.

First Lady Edith Wilson was a vigorous opponent of the women's suffrage movement. She called suffragettes agitating for the right to vote "detestable" and "disgusting." But while she didn't seem to think women should have the vote, she didn't have any problem with one running the White House—as long as it was she!

In October of 1919, President Woodrow Wilson had a stroke. He suffered major memory loss and could speak only with difficulty. Edith acted quickly to hide his condition from just about everyone. No one but the doctors could get in to see him. Even the vice president and secretary of state were turned away.

Then Mrs. Wilson took control.

During the five months the president was incapacitated, his wife screened everything he saw. She would meet with him in private, then come out and

issue orders. She penned directives to government officials that began, "The President says . . ." She even cowrote an inaugural message that went to Congress in his name.

She claimed she was just carrying out the president's wishes, but the truth is that he was nearly comatose much of the time.

Edith Wilson said she never made a single decision herself. But others saw it differently. The *Nashville Tennessean* described her as "the nation's first presidentess." The *Boston Globe* said her title should be "Acting First Man." And the *London Daily Mail* called her "the acting president of the United States"—a verdict with which it is hard to argue.

Vice President Thomas Riley Marshall was urged to undertake the duties of president during the crisis, but he refused. "I could throw this country into civil war by seizing the White House, but I won't," he told his wife.

Once Wilson was back on the job, he continued to need his wife's help to get through the day. He eventually recovered from the stroke, but never regained the vigor he had beforehand. He died just three years after leaving the White House.

WE HAVE PETTICOAT GOVERNMENT, MRS. WILSON IS PRESIDENT.

—SENATOR ALBERT FALL OF NEW MEXICO

THANK YOU FOR SMOKING

The hotel room that entered the history books.

George Harvey arrived at Chicago's Blackstone Hotel in June of 1920. He was there to attend the Republican National Convention. The prominent GOP leader from New York City checked into a spacious two-room suite. Harvey's name has faded from public memory, but the reception room of suite 404 was destined to become the most famous hotel room in American political history.

It was the original "smoke-filled room."

After four ballots, the convention found itself deadlocked between two presidential candidates, General Leonard Wood and Illinois governor Frank Lowden. A distant fourth in the balloting, out of the picture, really, was another candidate, Ohio senator Warren G. Harding.

Through the hot and sultry night that followed, a group of party leaders met in Harvey's room, looking for a way out of the deadlock. Bypassing the front-runners, they seized on the little-known Harding as the candidate least offensive to all. They summoned Harding and told the surprised candidate that they were all throwing their support behind him.

As the dawn broke, AP reporter Kirke Simpson filed a story saying, "Harding of Ohio was chosen by a group of men in a smoke-filled room early today." Harding went on to win the nomination and become president. And the "smoke-filled room"—describing a back room where political operators pull the strings out of public view—became an indispensable part of our political lexicon.

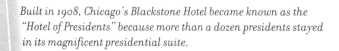

Built in 1908, Chicago's Blackstone Hotel became known as the "Hotel of Presidents" because more than a dozen presidents stayed in its magnificent presidential suite.

George Harvey ran Harper Publishing and was the managing director of Harper's Weekly. *Ten years earlier he was the man who convinced a college president named Woodrow Wilson to run for governor of New Jersey, thus putting Wilson on a road that would lead to the White House two years later.*

A political boss from Ohio who backed Harding was most likely the person who originated the phrase. Harry Daugherty predicted the outcome of the convention with amazing accuracy weeks before: "After the other candidates have gone their limit, some twelve to fifteen men, worn out and bleary-eyed for lack of sleep, will sit down around two o'clock in the morning, around a table in a smoke-filled room in some hotel, and decide the nomination. When that time comes, Harding will be selected."

THE TALKATIVE PRESIDENT

The secret side of the man called "Silent Cal."

Calvin Coolidge has gone down in history as perhaps our most dour and taciturn president. A famous story has a woman approaching him at a party and saying that she just bet a friend she could get Coolidge to say more than two words to her. "You lose," he supposedly replied.

But it turns out that "Silent Cal" could be pretty talkative.

Coolidge held regular press conferences twice a week for his entire presidency. Hundreds upon hundreds of them. Reporters submitted written questions, and the president talked about all sorts of things, often at great length. The public never knew it, because he forbade the press to quote him, or even mention that he was talking to them.

A White House stenographer took down everything, however, and the records turned up some forty years later. Coolidge comes across in them as playful, loquacious, and never at a loss for words—handling the press with a dry wit reminiscent of JFK forty years later.

Coolidge enjoyed give and take with White House correspondents. Quizzed one day about continuing reports that the secretary of war was going to resign, he responded with a burst of mock exasperation: "The secretary of war has not resigned. I don't expect he is going to, and I hope for the sake of his peace of mind that his resignation will not be reported in the future oftener than once in two weeks. I don't want to restrict the reporting but I think that would be often enough."

Going through his written questions one day: "I find that many are duplicates, or triplicates, or other cates." Talking about an upcoming trip: "I expect to spend a considerable part of it trying to amuse the newspapermen." Asked to sum up his presidency: "Perhaps one of the most important accomplishments of my administration has been minding my own business."

Add to that one other accomplishment—talking up a blue streak while maintaining a reputation for silence.

Coolidge's predecessor, Warren G. Harding, held similar off-the-record press conferences. It was during Harding's presidency that the press invented the term "White House spokesman" as a way to attribute the president's remarks.

Coolidge disarmed the press by asking their advice. Looking for a new secretary of the navy, he asked reporters if they had any suggestions—then promptly picked one of the names. Asked about his inaugural address, he said: "If any of you think of anything that ought to be covered, I should be obliged if you would suggest it."

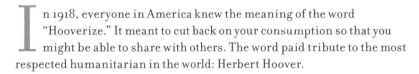

1929

THE NAME GAME

How one president's name came to stand for two very different things.

I n 1918, everyone in America knew the meaning of the word "Hooverize." It meant to cut back on your consumption so that you might be able to share with others. The word paid tribute to the most respected humanitarian in the world: Herbert Hoover.

Little more than a decade later, his name would take on a much darker meaning.

Hoover made millions as an engineer and businessman. After the outbreak of World War I, he turned his attention to humanitarian efforts. He organized a massive relief program to save millions in Europe from starvation. He convinced Americans to voluntarily conserve food with "Meatless Mondays" and "Wheatless Wednesdays" so that there would be plenty of food to share overseas.

Hoover's fame led him to the White House, and the tragic irony of his life.

A stock market crash in 1929 sent the nation's economy into a tailspin. Millions were thrown out of work. Many expected the great humanitarian to mount relief efforts. But Hoover was strongly opposed to government handouts. He seemed paralyzed in the face of disaster.

Soon shantytowns full of homeless people became known as "Hoovervilles." The newspapers they wrapped around themselves to keep warm were known as "Hoover blankets." The thin gruel handed out by soup kitchens was known as "Hoover soup."

A name that once stood for generosity and sharing had now become synonymous with poverty and despair.

Residents of a "Hooverville" that sprang up in Washington, D.C., in 1932

In 1919, Hoover's success at humanitarian efforts led a well-to-do New Yorker to say: "He is certainly a wonder and I wish we could make him President. . . . There could not be a better one." The man who spoke those words: Franklin Roosevelt, who would one day drive Hoover from the White House.

> **I CAN HOOVERIZE ON DINNERS, AND ON LIGHTS AND FUEL TOO, BUT I'LL NEVER LEARN TO HOOVERIZE WHEN IT COMES TO LOVING YOU.**
>
> —WORDS FROM A POPULAR WORLD WAR I–ERA SONG

Hoover's World War I relief efforts also gave him a great name overseas. In Finland, beef that came in humanitarian assistance packages was known as a *Hooverin pintaa*, which translates into "Hoover treat."

GOTTA GO!

Using the bathroom to advance your political career.

In 1931, a twenty-three-year-old schoolteacher from Texas came to Washington, D.C., for the first time. He was there to work as an aide to a newly elected representative from Texas, Richard Kleberg. He moved into the Dodge Hotel, where seventy-five other congressional aides also lived.

The young man knew nothing about how things worked on Capitol Hill. He was determined to change that in a hurry.

Everybody on his floor had to use one bathroom at the end of the hall. The young man went to take a shower, introducing himself to others using the bathroom. Then he came back half an hour later to take another shower, introducing himself to a different set of people. All in all he took four showers that night, meeting and making contact with as many congressional aides as possible. The following morning he went into the bathroom five different times to brush his teeth, shooting questions to everyone he met.

The young man's name was Lyndon Johnson. On his first day at the Dodge he was already demonstrating the unflagging energy that would help him master the ways of Congress and Washington. His multiple trips to the bathroom set him on the course that would lead him to become a congressman, a senator, and, more than thirty years later, president of the United States.

Johnson was the classic young man in a hurry. At lunch, he would try to be the first in line at the cafeteria so he could finish his food before the other people even sat down. That way he could devote his time to gathering information from his colleagues.

" THIS SKINNY BOY WAS AS GREEN AS ANYBODY COULD BE, BUT WITHIN A FEW MONTHS HE KNEW HOW TO OPERATE IN WASHINGTON BETTER THAN SOME WHO HAD BEEN HERE TWENTY YEARS. "

—CONGRESSIONAL SECRETARY ARTHUR PERRY

Six years after coming to Washington as a lowly staff man to a rookie Congressman, Johnson was himself elected to Congress at age twenty-nine.

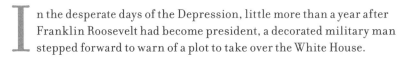

THE BUSINESS PLOT

The day Wall Street may have tried to overthrow the president.

In the desperate days of the Depression, little more than a year after Franklin Roosevelt had become president, a decorated military man stepped forward to warn of a plot to take over the White House.

Smedley Darlington Butler was a retired Marine Corps general who had twice won the Medal of Honor. Known as "Old Gimlet Eye," the colorful officer had a reputation for reckless bravery and blunt outspokenness. He told reporters that he had been approached by a group of Wall Street financiers to lead an army of five hundred thousand veterans on Washington to overthrow the government.

Leaders of the plot allegedly wanted to overthrow FDR because they thought the New Deal was an assault on capitalism. Butler said he was told that bigwigs J. P. Morgan and Grayson Murphy were ready to finance the plot with $3 million in cash, while corporate giants DuPont and Remington would supply the arms and ammunition. Once they had control of the capital, a "Secretary of General Welfare" would be appointed to run the country, reducing Roosevelt to a figurehead.

The supposed plotters ridiculed Butler's charges. The tale seemed far-fetched to many, and the media downplayed the story. But other officers said they had also been approached to take part. And the House Un-American Activities Committee took Butler's charges seriously enough to hold closed-door hearings, and issued a final report that largely supported the general.

So perhaps we ought to remember Smedley Darlington Butler as the man who saved the presidency.

The men supposedly involved in the plot all opposed FDR's New Deal and saw the president as a threat to laissez-faire capitalism.

Only five years earlier, twenty thousand veterans seeking money from Congress had marched on Washington and set up camp there. Butler had encouraged the "Bonus Army," which might have led to his being approached for the plot. According to Butler, middleman Gerald MacGuire told him: "You are the only fellow in America who can get the soldiers together."

After leaving the marines, Butler referred to his career as that of "a high-class muscleman for Wall Street and the big bankers. In short, I was a racketeer for capitalism."

" PERFECT MOONSHINE! TOO UNUTTERABLY RIDICULOUS TO COMMENT UPON. "

—THOMAS W. LAMONT, J. P. MORGAN'S PARTNER

PRESIDENTIAL PAYOFF

Which dead president would you rather have in your pocket?

Washington was a great man, but he's worth only a dollar at the bank. Lincoln will get you $5 and Grant will get you $50, but the real money is with some less famous presidents.

The $100 bill is currently the largest denomination being printed and distributed, but there used to be much bigger bills. The Treasury stopped distributing them in 1969, but these dead presidents are still legal tender today if you get your hands on one.

William McKinley is on the $500 bill.
Grover Cleveland is on the $1,000 bill.
James Madison is on the $5,000 bill.

They're all pikers, however, compared to President Woodrow Wilson. His face is on the largest and most unusual denomination of U.S. money ever printed.

The $100,000 bill.

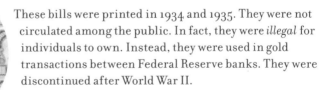

These bills were printed in 1934 and 1935. They were not circulated among the public. In fact, they were *illegal* for individuals to own. Instead, they were used in gold transactions between Federal Reserve banks. They were discontinued after World War II.

It may not be possible to say which of the presidents was the best. But there's no doubt at all about who was the most valuable.

The $100,000 bill was orange. All known pieces are in museums. Forty-two thousand of the bills were printed. If you had them all together, they would have a face value of $4.2 billion.

George Washington has the dubious honor of appearing on the smallest-denomination currency ever issued by the U.S. government: the three-cent note, which first came out in 1864. Notes smaller than $1 were issued between 1862 and 1876. They're known as "fractional currency."

THIRD-RATE BURGLARY

The break-in before the break-in.

The three Duke Law School students were all near the top of their class. Exams were over, and they were dying to see their final grades, which hadn't been made public yet. On the spur of the moment, they mounted a clandestine operation to obtain the information they sought.

A break-in.

In the hall outside the dean's office, two of the students hoisted the third up on their shoulders. He climbed through an open transom over the locked door. Once inside, he opened the door to his friends. Quickly they located keys to the dean's locked file drawer, got a peek at the grades and the final class rank, then slipped away as quietly as they came.

It was wrong, that's for sure—although the three young men regarded it as little more than a harmless prank.

For one of the students the break-in was an ironic foreshadowing of things to come. But next time he wouldn't be so lucky. At Duke he acquired the nickname "Gloomy Gus." Later he would get another moniker: "Tricky Dick." And while Richard Nixon got away with the break-in at the dean's office, the Watergate break-in would prove the undoing of his presidency.

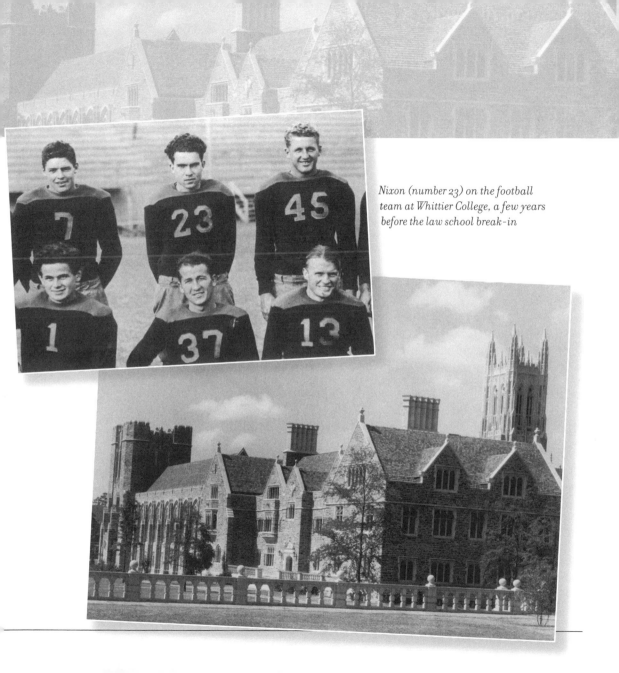

Nixon (number 23) on the football team at Whittier College, a few years before the law school break-in

DON'T MESS WITH THANKSGIVING!

A lesson one president had to learn the hard way.

I n 1939, Thanksgiving was scheduled to fall on the last day of November. Retailers lobbied President Franklin Roosevelt to move it one week earlier in order to lengthen the Christmas shopping season.

FDR wanted to do anything he could to help a still shaky economy, so he agreed. In the middle of August he casually announced to reporters that Thanksgiving would come a week early that year, and the next as well.

The decision quickly became front-page news, and it sparked a firestorm of controversy. The White House was flooded with letters, and cartoonists had a field day. Especially aggrieved were calendar makers, whose products were suddenly inaccurate, and high school football coaches upset to find that the big Thanksgiving game was no longer on the right day.

The issue divided the country. Twenty-three states decided to celebrate on the original date, while twenty-three others went along with the new date proclaimed by Roosevelt. Texas and Colorado, unable to decide, celebrated both.

The following year Roosevelt sheepishly admitted that the whole thing was a mistake, and returned Thanksgiving to its original date. Congress passed a law setting that date in stone, so that no president could ever again mess with Thanksgiving.

Shinnston, W. Va.
August 15, 1939

The President
White House
Washington, D. C.

Mr. President:

I see by the paper this morning where you
want to change Thanksgiving Day to
November 23 of.which I heartily approve.
Thanks.

Now, there are some things that I would
like done and would appreciate your
approval:

1. Have Sunday changed to
   Wednesday;

2. Have Monday's to be
   Christmas;

3. Have it strictly against
   the Will of God to work
   on Tuesday;

4. Have Thursday to be Pay
   Day with time and one-half
   for overtime;

5. Require everyone to take
   Friday and Saturday off
   for a fishing trip down
   the Potomac.

With these in view and hoping you will give
me some consideration at your next Congress,
I remain

               Yours very truly

               Shelby O. Bennett
               SHELBY O. BENNETT

SOB:jas

Many letter writers mocked what they saw as a perfect example of FDR's high-handedness. Others who complained to the president included couples with Thanksgiving wedding plans and children with Thanksgiving birthdays.

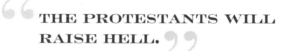

THE PROTESTANTS WILL RAISE HELL.

President Roosevelt seriously considered moving Thanksgiving to a Monday to give workers a three-day weekend, but reluctantly dropped the idea when aides convinced him that religious leaders wouldn't go for it.

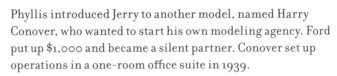

MODEL J. FORD

How does it feel to be one of the beautiful people?

Jerry Ford may seem like the least glamorous of all modern presidents. He was the personification of a square Midwesterner. But as a young man he was not only a successful New York model, he also helped found one of the hottest modeling agencies in the country.

While attending Yale Law School, Ford started dating a beautiful coed named Phyllis Brown. In 1939 she dropped out of school and started modeling in New York. She quickly became very popular, frequently appearing on the covers of various magazines. She got her good-looking boyfriend into the business as well. Ford modeled for several magazine spreads, and even appeared on the cover of *Cosmopolitan*.

Phyllis introduced Jerry to another model, named Harry Conover, who wanted to start his own modeling agency. Ford put up $1,000 and became a silent partner. Conover set up operations in a one-room office suite in 1939.

The Conover Modeling Agency soon became one of the country's most successful modeling agencies, grossing millions a year. Had he chosen to, Ford undoubtedly could have married Phyllis and made a career in the modeling business.

But the bright lights of New York held no allure for Ford. After graduating from law school he left the city, the modeling business, and Phyllis behind. He returned to Grand Rapids, Michigan, there to set off on the long and winding road that would take him one day to the White House.

Phyllis and Jerry appeared in Look *magazine in 1940 in a spread entitled "A Weekend in the Life of the Beautiful People." Critics later joked that Jerry Ford was too dumb to talk and chew gum at the same time. But at Yale he did manage to attend law school, coach football and boxing, date Phyllis, and pursue modeling all at the same time.*

Ford thought Phyllis was the love of his life—until after World War II, when he met a divorcée named Elizabeth Bloomer in Grand Rapids. They had something in common— Betty too had once worked as a fashion model in New York.

Harry Conover is credited with inventing the term "cover girl." He promoted "the kind of natural, well-scrubbed girl you used to take to the junior prom." As World War II was drawing to a close, he encouraged his models to chow down: "Eat as much as you want," he said; "returning servicemen want a good well-rounded bundle, not a matchstick."

LIGHTS ON

FDR and night baseball

After the United States entered World War II, baseball commissioner Kenesaw Mountain Landis wrote to President Franklin Roosevelt asking if major league baseball should go ahead with the forthcoming baseball season.

Roosevelt replied with what has become known as the "green-light letter," telling baseball owners, "It would be best for the country to keep baseball going." He explained that he thought baseball offered a valuable recreational outlet for a nation committing itself to an all-out war effort. Almost as an aside, FDR offered a suggestion. "Incidentally, I hope that night games can be extended because it gives an opportunity to the day shift to see a game occasionally."

Those words had a profound effect on the game of baseball.

Up to this time, each team was limited to seven night games. Many owners strongly opposed increasing that number, but in response to the president's suggestion, they doubled the limit to fourteen for each team. The following season, the American League removed the limit entirely. Some teams played more than forty night games a season.

The expansion of night baseball was a home run. Night games were better attended than day games. Nevertheless, after the war ended, many team owners advocated returning to the prewar limits. When they deadlocked on the question, the new baseball commissioner, Albert "Happy" Chandler, had to make the call. He ruled teams could play ball under the lights as often as they liked.

The war was over. FDR was dead. But night baseball was here to stay.

THE WHITE HOUSE
WASHINGTON

January 15, 1942.

My dear Judge:-

            Thank you for yours of January fourteenth. As
you will, of course, realize the final decision about the
baseball season must rest with you and the Baseball Club
owners -- so what I am going to say is solely a personal
and not an official point of view.

            I honestly feel that it would be best for the
country to keep baseball going. There will be fewer people
unemployed and everybody will work longer hours and harder
than ever before.

            And that means that they ought to have a
chance for recreation and for taking their minds off
their work even more than before.

            Baseball provides a recreation which does
not last over two hours or two hours and a half, and
which can be got for very little cost. And, incidentally,
I hope that night games can be extended because it gives
an opportunity to the day shift to see a game occasionally.

            As to the players themselves, I know you agree
with me that individual players who are of active military
or naval age should go, without question, into the services.
Even if the actual quality of the teams is lowered by the
greater use of older players, this will not dampen the
popularity of the sport. Of course, if any individual
has some particular aptitude in a trade or profession,
he ought to serve the Government. That, however, is a
matter which I know you can handle with complete justice.

            Here is another way of looking at it -- if
300 teams use 5,000 or 6,000 players, these players are
a definite recreational asset to at least 20,000,000
of their fellow citizens -- and that in my judgment is
thoroughly worthwhile.

            With every best wish,

                        Very sincerely yours,

                              Franklin D Roosevelt

Hon. Kenesaw M. Landis,
333 North Michigan Avenue,
Chicago,
Illinois.

*A big baseball fan, FDR also had a role
in the very first major league baseball
game played under the lights, back
in 1935. The president threw a switch
in Washington, turning on the big
arc lights six hundred miles away at
Crosley Field in Cincinnati, where the
Reds beat the Phillies 2-1.*

The Chicago Cubs had planned to install lights at Wrigley
Field in 1942, but with the outbreak of war, the team
decided instead to donate the lights to the federal government.
In 1944 the Cubs were denied permission to install lights
because of wartime shortages of critical material. And so
began, quite by accident, the tradition of no night baseball at
Wrigley. Lights were not installed there until 1988, and even
today the team plays only a limited number of night games.

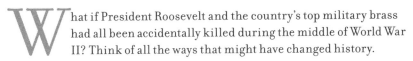

CLOSE CALL OF THE *PORTER*

The friendly fire that almost changed the course of World War II.

What if President Roosevelt and the country's top military brass had all been accidentally killed during the middle of World War II? Think of all the ways that might have changed history.

Truth is—it almost happened.

On November 14, 1943, FDR and his chief military advisers were secretly crossing the Atlantic aboard the USS *Iowa* on their way to an Allied summit meeting in Tehran. Tremendous care was taken to hide the identity of the VIPs in order to assure their safety.

Suddenly a torpedo was seen heading straight for the *Iowa*. Everyone aboard thought they were under attack from a German submarine. But in fact, the torpedo came from an American ship.

The escort destroyer USS *William D. Porter* had accidentally fired the torpedo during a drill. As danger alarms went off and crewmen headed to battle stations, the battleship *Iowa* maneuvered sharply and avoided the torpedo, which exploded just a hundred yards off the stern. The force of the explosion rocked the *Iowa* so violently that one officer aboard shouted, "My God, he hit us!" But the ship was not harmed at all.

History records a successful summit that helped secure an Allied victory. But there could have been a very different outcome—if not for a near miss.

After the incident, the USS Porter was escorted to Bermuda, where the entire crew was placed under arrest. "You never saw so many people coming and going, interrogations all night long," says former crewman Bob Jones. The captain was transferred to a desk job and the Porter was ordered to the Aleutian Islands. It is said that after that other ships often hailed her with the greeting "Don't shoot—we're Republicans!"

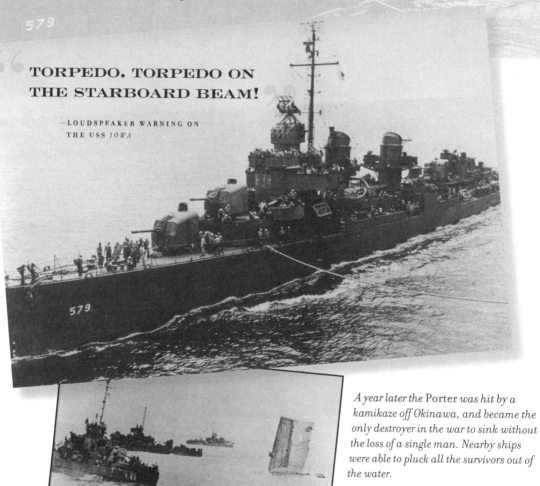

"TORPEDO, TORPEDO ON THE STARBOARD BEAM!

—LOUDSPEAKER WARNING ON THE USS *IOWA*

A year later the Porter was hit by a kamikaze off Okinawa, and became the only destroyer in the war to sink without the loss of a single man. Nearby ships were able to pluck all the survivors out of the water.

WHERE DOES IT STOP?

Passing the buck from a prison paint shop to the Oval Office.

I n the fall of 1945, a burly federal marshal named Fred Canfil paid a visit to a federal prison in El Reno, Oklahoma. As he was talking to warden L. Clark Schilder, a sign on the warden's desk caught his attention. Canfil made an admiring comment about the sign, and mentioned that he thought a friend of his would just love it.

No problem, said the warden. The head of the prison's paint shop had designed the sign, and it would be easy enough to have him run up another. Warden Schilder promised to send the duplicate sign to Canfil as soon as possible, and he was as good as his word.

Fred Canfil was a lifelong political hack once described by an associate as "loudmouthed, profane, vulgar, and uncouth." But on this day he made a contribution to popular culture and presidential lore that will live forever.

Canfil's longtime friend was fellow Missourian Harry Truman, who had become president just a few months before. The sign he gave to the president contained four words that would become a part of Truman's legacy:

"The Buck Stops Here."

The sign made quite an impact given that it was on the president's desk only a short time. It was put on display at the Truman Presidential Museum in 1957, and has been a favorite of visitors ever since.

66 **THE PRESIDENT—WHOEVER HE IS—HAS TO DECIDE. HE CAN'T PASS THE BUCK TO ANYBODY. NO ONE ELSE CAN DO THE DECIDING FOR HIM. THAT'S HIS JOB.** 99

—HARRY TRUMAN

The expression comes from the phrase "passing the buck," which in turn comes from frontier poker playing. The buck was a marker showing who had the next deal. If somebody didn't want the responsibility of the deal, he could "pass the buck" to the person on his left. Sometimes a silver dollar was used as the marker—which is where we get the slang word "buck" for a dollar.

1947

JACK'S FIRST WIFE

Did JFK secretly marry someone else before he married Jackie?

In January of 1947, Massachusetts congressman Jack Kennedy was a swinging bachelor vacationing in Florida. He was spending a lot of time with a twice-divorced Palm Beach socialite named Durie Malcolm. "The two were inseparable," according to the *New York World Telegram*'s society writer. Early one morning he and Durie were married by a justice of the peace.

Or so the story goes.

The tale first surfaced in 1961. Many dismissed it as mere rumor. There was, however, a piece of documentary proof: the so-called Blauvelt genealogy, a carefully compiled private history of one of America's oldest families, which reported the marriage as fact.

Once the story broke in the media, the White House issued firm denials. Kennedy leaned heavily on his friend Ben Bradlee, then an editor at *Newsweek*, to help discredit the tale. Durie Malcolm stoutly denied it then, and continued to deny it ever afterward.

...al that I was talki...
...eceived a copy and said i...
...me individual is sending it out...
...ncerned me. The Attorney Gener...
...rn and said he supposed they will alw...
I just wanted him to be alert to this.

John Edgar Hoover
Director

But after more than fifty years of silence, Kennedy family friend Charles Spalding told investigative reporter Seymour Hersh that it did indeed happen. "You must be nuts," he says he told his friend at the time. According to Spalding, family patriarch Joe Kennedy demanded that the whole thing be hushed up for fear that marriage outside the Catholic Church to a divorcée would kill his son's career in politics. Spalding says he and an attorney removed the records from the courthouse and destroyed them.

55 PM   O.C.   November 22, 1961

MEMORANDUM FOR PERSONAL FILES

The Attorney General called ...
he had seen this thing being circulated
esident. The Attorney General stated

Many Kennedy intimates believe there was such a marriage, and that he really loved her. Did it really happen? It all depends on whom you choose to believe.

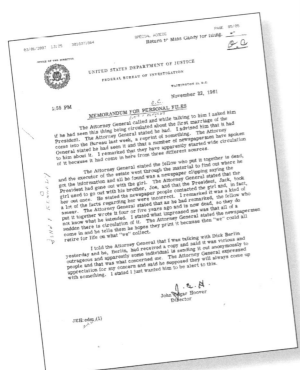

If the story is true and the marriage was never legally dissolved, that would mean that Kennedy's marriage to Jacqueline Bouvier was not a legal one, and their children were, legally speaking, illegitimate.

FIRST DEBATE

A practice round for a presidential showdown.

When John Kennedy and Richard Nixon squared off for their historic presidential debates in 1960, they knew something most of the country didn't.

They had debated before.

Thirteen years earlier, in 1947, both Nixon and Kennedy were freshmen congressmen, still wet behind the ears. They were invited to the industrial town of McKeesport, Pennsylvania, to debate the Taft-Hartley Bill, a Republican-sponsored measure designed to limit the power of labor unions.

No one in the hotel ballroom that night knew that the debate was a glimpse into the future.

Ever the fighter, Nixon was aggressive in arguing for the bill. A member of his college debate team, he challenged his opponent on every point. Union members in the audience booed and jeered him, but he kept on nonetheless. Kennedy, ever the charmer, often ignored his opponent as he sought middle ground and tried to win over the crowd.

The debate was ruled a draw.

Later that night, the two men took a night train for Washington. They drew straws for the lower berth, and Nixon won. It was the last time he was to beat Kennedy in anything.

THE DAILY NEWS

April 22, 1947

Tuesday Evening

-ws Section
-ed, financial news, stock
-ure stories, comics and

Sports, q
quotations,
general new

Maps Battle on Proposed Legislation Curbing

Congressmen Debate Merits of House-Passed Labor Bill; Nixon Sees Rights Protected, Kennedy Fears Civil Strife

Republican, Democrat Air Views During Junto Forum

Two of the nation's youngest Congressmen predicted opposite effects of stringent labor legislation, now undergone Senate study, during a Junto forum last night at the Penn McKee Hotel.

The Hartley Bill, which recently passed the House, upholds the fundamental rights of the working man, Representative Richard M. Nixon, Republican, California, declared.

The bill would "fire the first shot in a war to end labor peace," Representative John F. Kennedy, Democrat, Massachusetts, contended in opposition.

First-Termers

The opinions of the two first-termers, both World War II Vet-

the bill Congressman Nixon stated that the fundamental rights of labor would not be usurped.

Kennedy Replies

Congressman Kennedy in rebuttal, questioned the protection of the working man by the bill. He declared.

Russia Keeps News Promise

Censorship Withheld All 'Big 4' Reports

By International News Service
MOSCOW, April 22—M
the news out of Moscow
class is bad press, as ii
ness is to be free to send
A hundred foreign corre
ent are filing 10,000 word
about the Council of Foreign
isters, without suffering a
deletion from the censor's red

reported Fully

U. S. Awaits Quirino Visit

Official of Philippines Sets Vital Parleys

By International News Service
WASHINGTON, April 22—Diplomatic quarters today foresee a series of important United States-Philippine relations during the forthcoming visit of Philippine Vice President Elpidio Quirino. Quirino's projected visit to Washington as the official guest of the United States Government had been forecast long following the inability of President Roxas to make the trip.

Nixon was thirty-four and Kennedy twenty-nine at the time of their first debate. Afterward they had dinner at the Star Diner, and others there marveled at how well the two men seemed to hit it off.

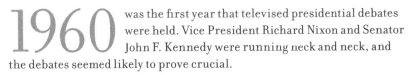

MAKEUP MOMENT

Did a cosmetics choice change the course of a presidential election?

1960 was the first year that televised presidential debates were held. Vice President Richard Nixon and Senator John F. Kennedy were running neck and neck, and the debates seemed likely to prove crucial.

CBS was televising the first debate from a TV station in Chicago. Wanting everything to go right, the network flew in one of television's best makeup artists, Frances Arnold, to make sure that each candidate looked his best under the hot lights.

Today it is commonplace for politicians to wear makeup on television, but that wasn't the case in 1960. When Kennedy, tanned from a West Coast trip, said no to makeup, Nixon also refused. He apparently thought it would damage his image if it got out that he was wearing makeup and Kennedy wasn't.

Bad call.

Back in the privacy of their dressing rooms, each candidate got a hurried makeup job from an adviser. One of Nixon's assistants put something called Shave Stick on him. Kennedy's aide dabbed some Max Factor Crème Puff on the candidate's face. When they came out, Kennedy looked great. Nixon looked terrible.

People who listened to the debate on radio thought Nixon won, but the 60 million who saw it on television overwhelmingly considered JFK the victor. He went on to win one of the closest elections in history, with Max Factor being a critical factor in his victory.

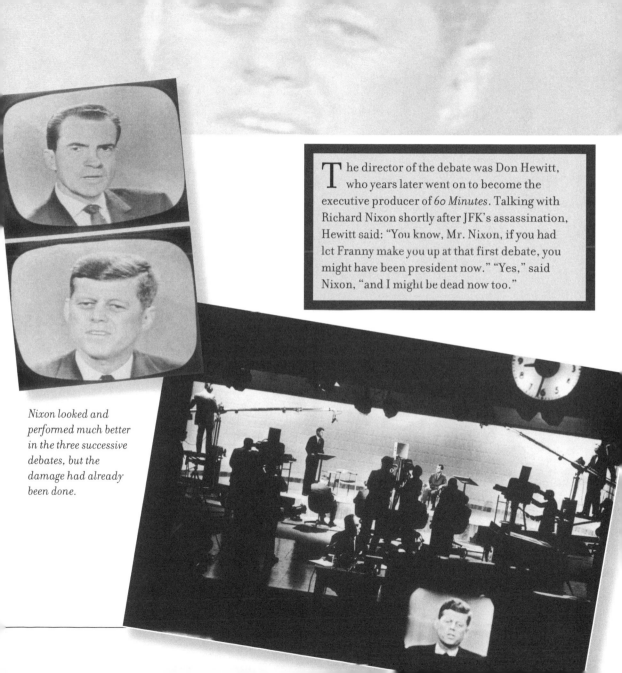

The director of the debate was Don Hewitt, who years later went on to become the executive producer of *60 Minutes*. Talking with Richard Nixon shortly after JFK's assassination, Hewitt said: "You know, Mr. Nixon, if you had let Franny make you up at that first debate, you might have been president now." "Yes," said Nixon, "and I might be dead now too."

Nixon looked and performed much better in the three successive debates, but the damage had already been done.

ICH BIN EIN BERLINER

The story behind the famous speech.

Y ou've probably never heard of Robert Lochner. But he played a part in creating one of the most memorable lines ever uttered by an American president.

Lochner was an American who grew up in Germany before World War II, and went back afterward to work for the American government there. He was a fluent German speaker and an obvious choice as a translator when President John F. Kennedy came to visit in 1963.

Lochner came to the States to help JFK prepare for the trip, and tried to teach him several German phrases. But Kennedy's pronunciation was terrible, so he decided not to attempt any German speaking on the trip.

"Let's leave foreign languages to the distaff side," he said, referring to his wife's fluency in French.

The president changed his mind when he got to Berlin, where he was to give a speech within sight of the Berlin Wall. As his entourage walked up the steps of the city hall, he called Lochner over and asked him to write out a single phrase in German. It was from the speech he was about to give, designed to express his solidarity with beleaguered West Berliners. Lochner wrote it out phonetically, and coached the president on how to say it. Then Kennedy went out and gave a speech that would live in memory forever . . . largely because of that one line.

"If you ever heard the tape, it wasn't exactly perfect," Lochner recalled, "but with those few words you couldn't go wrong."

After rehearsing with Lochner, JFK wrote the phrase phonetically on the back of his speech card.

> **ALL FREE MEN, WHEREVER THEY MAY LIVE, ARE CITIZENS OF BERLIN, AND, THEREFORE, AS A FREE MAN, I TAKE PRIDE IN THE WORDS *'ICH BIN EIN BERLINER!'***
>
> —JOHN F. KENNEDY, JUNE 26, 1963

Robert Lochner (center) translates for President Kennedy.

Because there is a jelly-filled German pastry known as a Berliner, an urban myth has sprung up that what Kennedy actually said was, "I am a jelly doughnut." Linguists dismiss the idea, affirming that he made his point correctly. Clearly the crowd, which greeted his words with a thundering and ecstatic cheer, knew exactly what he was saying.

THE NIGHT THE LIGHTS WENT ON IN GEORGIA

A close encounter of the presidential kind.

It was just after dark that a dozen men in the small town of Leary, Georgia, saw a strange light in the sky. Most of the men were members of the Leary Lions Club, getting ready to go into their monthly meeting. One was an out-of-towner, an up-and-coming politician who had come to speak to the club. Fascinated by what he saw in the sky, he made a beeline for his tape recorder and dictated details into it because he thought it was such a "remarkable sight."

That man was Jimmy Carter, who remains the first and only president of the United States to officially report a UFO sighting.

Four years later, while governor of Georgia, Carter filled out a form documenting his sighting. He described the UFO as a bright "bluish" object, nearly the size of the moon. He estimated it was no more than a thousand yards away. He said it seemed to move away, turning reddish in color as it did so. Then it came back closer before finally departing.

Skeptics have suggested that the object Carter saw was the planet Venus, or perhaps the town's silver water tower. Carter apparently believed differently. "I don't laugh at people anymore when they say they've seen UFOs," he said a few years later. "I've seen one myself."

IN CONNECTION WITH THIS REPORT,
CITIZENS TO REPORT SIMILAR
REFER, WE WILL KEEP YOUR NAME
KING THE PROPER STATEMENT BELOW,
FORM, FOR OUR OWN CONFIDENTIAL.

E KEEP MY NAME CONFIDENTIAL.
TURE:
~ Jimmy Carter

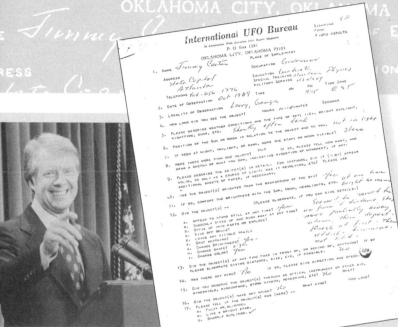

Carter's presidency saw a rise in UFO interest due to the release of Star Wars and Close Encounters. UFOlogists hoped that Carter would blow the lid off what they saw as a government cover-up on the subject of UFOs. But after he was inaugurated, Carter became virtually mum on the subject.

> " I HAVE NO IDEA WHAT IT WAS. . . . I THINK IT WAS A LIGHT BECKONING ME TO RUN IN THE CALIFORNIA PRIMARY. "
>
> —CARTER, MAKING FUN OF HIS OWN EXPERIENCE WHILE RUNNING FOR PRESIDENT

During the Carter administration, the prime minister of Grenada asked the U.N. to create an agency to investigate UFO reports. The General Assembly passed a resolution encouraging member countries to study the subject, but declined to go into the UFO business itself.

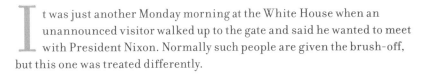

THE KING AND I

One of the most bizarre White House meetings ever.

It was just another Monday morning at the White House when an unannounced visitor walked up to the gate and said he wanted to meet with President Nixon. Normally such people are given the brush-off, but this one was treated differently.

It was "The King." Elvis Presley.

The famous singer dropped off a six-page handwritten letter requesting a meeting. Nixon adviser H. R. Haldeman decided to give him an appointment with the president the very same day.

Their brief get-together in the Oval Office may be one of the oddest moments in the Nixon presidency. Presley told the president earnestly that he had been studying Communist brainwashing and the drug culture for over a decade. He asked Nixon to make him a "Federal Agent at Large" to help fight the spread of drugs (especially ironic given that Presley was a chronic drug abuser who eventually died of an overdose).

He also offered the surprising observation that the Beatles were a major source of anti-American spirit, and their music was filled with anti-American themes.

As the meeting drew to a close, Presley seemed gripped by emotion as he told the president that he was "on your side." Then he surprised the normally aloof Nixon by giving him a bear hug.

The next thing you know, Elvis had left the building.

AmericanAirlines

In Flight…
Altitude: 0
Location:

Dear Mr. President:

First I would like to introduce myself. I am Elvis Presley and admire you and Have Great Respect for your office. I talked to Vice President Agnew in Palm Springs 3 weeks ago and expressed my concern for our country. The Drug Culture, the Hippie Elements, the SDS, Black Panthers, etc. do not consider me as their enemy or as they call it the Establishment. I call it America...

CONFIDENTIAL
Atten. President Nixon
Via Sen. George Murphy
from
Elvis Presley

PHONE ME 85900
RM. 505-506
UNDER THE NAME
OF JON BURROWS

Presley scrawled his letter requesting an appointment with the president while on a cross-country flight.

I n response to Presley's request, the White House arranged for him to get a Bureau of Narcotics badge with his name on it.

LEGACY LOST

The father the
Internet never had.

Nowhere in the history of the Internet is the name H. R. Haldeman mentioned. But if not for Watergate, things might have been very different. And the Internet might have burst upon us years earlier.

Way back in 1973, the chief of staff to President Nixon was planning a major initiative for what he referred to as the "Wired Nation." Haldeman hoped it would be the jewel of Nixon's second term. But Watergate soon consumed the Nixon White House, and the idea came to nothing. Haldeman talked about what might have been shortly after Nixon resigned in 1974.

"Through computer . . . you could order whatever you wanted. The morning paper, entertainment services, shopping services, coverage of sporting events and public events. Technologically it can be done." It was going to happen anyway, Haldeman predicted. "But if I had stayed on for the second term, I believe it would have come much faster."

Haldeman's words showed astonishing foresight, since the Internet as we know it today lay a decade or two in the future. With major federal backing in the seventies, it might have materialized much more quickly. And instead of being reviled as the architects of the Watergate cover-up, Richard Nixon and H. R. Haldeman might today be hailed as the visionary leaders who helped create the Net.

More than a decade before people started using the phrase "information superhighway," Haldeman and Nixon were tossing around that idea as well. "Just as Eisenhower linked up the nation's cities by highways," said Haldeman, "the Nixon legacy would have them linked by cable."

The politician most associated with the Internet is Al Gore, who endured national ridicule for telling an interviewer in 1999, "During my service in the United States Congress, I took the initiative in creating the Internet." Gore did, in fact, help pass legislation in the late 1980s that helped the Internet move dramatically forward.

Ever wonder who had the first computer on the Internet? This is it. Known as the IMP 1, it was installed in Dr. Len Kleinrock's UCLA laboratory in September of 1969. A second computer was installed at Stanford a month later. On October 29 of that year, technicians got the two machines talking to each other, and ARPANET, the predecessor to the Internet, was born.

INTERFACE MESSAGE PROCESSOR

PANDORA'S BOX

The most bizarre assassination attempt in American history.

I t was a few minutes after seven at Baltimore-Washington International, and passengers were lining up to get on an early morning Delta flight for Atlanta. Suddenly a burly man ran up to the gate, shot the security guard dead, and then ran down the ramp to the waiting plane.

More than twenty-five years before al-Qaeda got the idea, Samuel Byck was carrying out his plan to hijack a jetliner and crash into the White House.

The forty-four-year-old Philadelphia man had convinced himself that President Nixon was the cause of all his problems. Turning suicidal, he concocted a plan he called "Project Pandora's Box." He recorded the details on hours of audiotapes that he made beforehand. "When the plane is in this position, I will shoot the pilot and then in the last few minutes try to steer the plane into the target, which is the White House."

Byck's plan never got off the ground. Once aboard the plane he killed the copilot and wounded the pilot, then was himself wounded by policemen firing through the window. He killed himself before he was captured.

Byck viewed himself as a political terrorist, and said on one of his tapes: "It's very unfortunate that a good wholesome guy like me has to kill himself or get killed to make a point."

But exactly what that point was, nobody was ever sure.

Byck was arrested twice for demonstrating in front of the White House without a permit, and was even questioned by the Secret Service for allegedly making threatening remarks about the president.

> **ONE MAN'S TERRORIST IS ANOTHER MAN'S PATRIOT . . . IT ALL DEPENDS ON WHICH SIDE OF THE FENCE YOU HAPPEN TO BE ON AT THE TIME.**
>
> —SAMUEL BYCK, IN AN AUDIOTAPE HE MADE BEFORE THE ASSASSINATION ATTEMPT

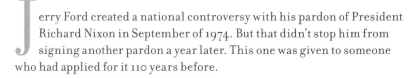

PRESIDENTIAL PARDON

The pardon
President Ford
isn't famous for.

Jerry Ford created a national controversy with his pardon of President Richard Nixon in September of 1974. But that didn't stop him from signing another pardon a year later. This one was given to someone who had applied for it 110 years before.

Civil War general Robert E. Lee.

After the Civil War had ended, any Confederate soldier could apply for pardon and have his citizenship restored. General Lee decided to do just that. He sent his application to General Grant, who recommended to President Andrew Johnson that it be approved.

For that to happen, Lee had to take a notarized oath of allegiance to the Union. Such a move was considered controversial in a South still not reconciled to its defeat. But Lee went ahead and did it, wanting to set an example that others would follow to help heal the wounds of war.

Lee's oath of allegiance was forwarded to the secretary of state. But instead of passing it on to the president, he gave it to a friend as a souvenir—perhaps purposely wanting to derail Lee's application. General Lee died in 1870 without receiving a pardon or having his citizenship restored.

One hundred years after his death, Lee's oath turned up in the National Archives. Congress voted to pardon Lee and restore his citizenship. President Ford signed the bill into law. And an oversight 110 years old was corrected.

Ford signed Lee's pardon at Arlington House, the prewar home of Lee that is now part of Arlington Cemetery. Robert E. Lee IV and Robert E. Lee V were present for the signing.

The pardon of General Lee was not without controversy, though on a far smaller scale than was the case with Nixon's pardon. John Conyers, an African American representative from Michigan, called it "neither healing nor charitable." Other congressmen suggested that Vietnam draft dodgers should be pardoned before Lee.

THE CODE OF
THE SERVICE

*The movie that
saved a president's
life.*

In 1939, Ronald Reagan made a film called *Code of the Secret Service*. It was one of a series of movies in which he played a tough-guy Secret Service agent named Brass Bancroft. It wasn't one of Reagan's more memorable pictures. He said more than once that it was the worst film he ever made.

But he ended up being very glad he made it.

The film captured the imagination of a ten-year-old boy in Miami, Florida. "I made my dad take me to that movie quite a few times," recalled Jerry Parr. He vowed that when he grew up, he would become a Secret Service agent himself. And so he did.

Forty-two years later, on March 30, 1981, Secret Service agent Jerry Parr was part of the detail guarding President Reagan when assassin John Hinckley opened fire. It was Parr who braved the hail of bullets to tackle Reagan and push him into the waiting car, which sped off toward the White House. And it was Parr who saw Reagan coughing up blood, and made the split-second decision to head straight for the hospital. Unbeknownst to either of them, a ricocheting bullet had sliced into Reagan's chest, causing massive internal bleeding. Parr's decision to seek immediate medical care saved the president's life.

Brass Bancroft could have done no better.

Reagan, with Parr on his right, moments before the shooting. All four people hit are in this picture: the president, press secretary James Brady, policeman Tom Delehanty, and Secret Service agent Tim McCarthy.

Despite losing more than half the blood in his body and coming within a whisker of death, the president still got off some memorable quips. "I hope you're a Republican," he told a doctor about to operate. "Honey, I forgot to duck," he explained to his wife, Nancy.

This is to certify that

is a member of the

The owner of this card promises to be on the lookout for dangerous spies and to follow the thrilling exploits of the secret service on the screen at the

[THEATRE IMPRINT]

JR. SECRET SERVICE

OPERATIVE No. 666

Ronald Reagan
Chief of Jr. Secret Service

Kids who went to the 1939 movie were given cards like this one.

ANATOMY OF A GREAT LINE

Sometimes it can be very complicated to say something very simple.

I t started with Ingeborg Elz. The Berlin woman was hosting a dinner party for White House speechwriter Peter Robinson, who was researching a speech Ronald Reagan was going to give at the Berlin Wall. Talking about Soviet premier Mikhail Gorbachev, she said if he was serious about *perestroika,* "he can prove it. He can get rid of this wall."

Robinson seized on the idea as the cornerstone for the speech. Then came writer's block. He couldn't get the line the way he wanted it. "Herr Gorbachev, bring down this wall." The "Herr" was to please his German audience. But it didn't quite work. "Herr Gorbachev, *take* down this wall." Still not right. He even tried taking the whole line out, replacing it with a challenge, in German, to open the Brandenburg Gate: *"Herr Gorbachev, machen Sie dieses Tor auf."* Not exactly a line to resonate through the ages.

Eventually he got it right. Then it turned out that everybody seemed to hate it. Secretary of State George Schulz, National Security Adviser Colin Powell, and others declared that it was too provocative, that it should be taken out. News drafts of the speech were written with the line taken out. The point was argued for weeks, right up to the day of the speech.

One man never wavered in his support of the phrase: the president. The line stayed in. And less than three years later, the wall came down.

Opposition to the line was so fierce that Deputy White House Chief of Staff Ken Duberstein decided that it was up to the president to make the final call. That led to this memorable exchange:

Reagan: *I'm the president, aren't I?*
Duberstein: *Yes sir, Mr. President. We're clear about that.*
Reagan: *So I get to decide whether the line about tearing down the wall stays in?*
Duberstein: *That's right, sir. It's your decision.*
Reagan: *Then it stays in.*

 MR. GORBACHEV, TEAR DOWN THIS WALL.

—RONALD REAGAN, JUNE 12, 1987, AT THE BERLIN WALL

OLD MAN'S VOTE

It's never too late to vote for the first time.

The old man had never voted. He was seventy-five years old, and he had never voted in one of his country's elections. Not for president, or mayor, or anything.

He had been very involved in public service during his long life. He founded youth groups, worked in community organizations, did some writing. He had lots of friends, many children and grandchildren. But he had never voted in an election.

Then, in his seventy-sixth year, he cast his ballot for the first time ever.

If the story ended here, it would be a simple, heartwarming tale of a man who late in life discovered what a wonderful feeling it is to exercise the right to vote. But this story is much more than that—for two reasons.

The old man lived in South Africa. And the reason he had never exercised the right to vote was that he was black, and his country had never given him that right. Now, at long last, for the first time in his life, he was allowed to vote.

What a powerful feeling it must have been.

Perhaps even more powerful than we can imagine. Because when the old man voted for the very first time, he voted for himself. For president. In the knowledge that millions of others, also voting for the first time, would do the same—thus making this old man, Nelson Mandela, the first black president of South Africa, a country that had never allowed blacks to vote until that day.

Another prisoner who became president was Václav Havel. The Czech playwright was imprisoned numerous times for his political activities, once serving four years in jail. After leading the "Velvet Revolution" that ended Communist rule of Czechoslovakia in 1989, he became the last president of Czechoslovakia, and the first president of the new Czech Republic.

Mandela spent twenty-eight years in prison, much of it in this cell in the notorious Robben Island prison. Released in 1990, he was elected president four years later in the first South African election in which blacks were allowed to vote.

SEEING RED AND BLUE

How political color-coding became part of our self-image.

It's become a familiar form of shorthand: red states and blue states. Red states, of course, vote Republican. Blue states go Democratic. But the expression also conjures up a cultural and geographic divide. Red-staters, according to the stereotype, dwell in the heartland and love NASCAR and country music. Blue-staters inhabit the coasts and big cities, sipping lattes and reading the *New York Times*.

Where, oh where did it all begin?

In the 1870s, Texas color-coded its ballots to help Spanish-speaking voters make sense of them. The Democrats were the Blues, the Republicans were the Reds.

In 1972, NBC News executive Gordon Manning introduced the color-coded electoral map to election night coverage. Other networks followed suit, but there was randomness to it. One network might use blue for Democrats, while another used red.

By 1996 the major networks had informally agreed to use red for the Republicans and blue for the Democrats. Then came the 2000 presidential election between George Bush and Al Gore. The nation stared at those electoral maps, not just for a day or two, but for week after week as the two sides argued over who had won. The maps suggested a regional and cultural divide as well as a political one, and the color-coding began to imprint itself on the national consciousness.

A week after the election, comedian David Letterman offered a compromise: "Let's make George W. Bush president of the red states and Al Gore head of the blue ones."

And soon the whole nation was seeing red . . . and blue.

One of the first uses of the color code in a cultural sense came from NBC anchor Brian Williams, writing in *Time* about the death of Dale Earnhardt in March of 2001. "Millions of Americans, mostly in the red states, if you recall your election charts, lost a hero the instant the black car veered violently into the wall."

NBC's election map in 2000 filled up with red states for Bush and blue for Gore. Historically, red has been associated with the left—as in calling Communists "Reds"—and blue with the right. On election night in 1976 Jerry Ford shouted "Go Blue," the old Michigan cheer, as the network election map coded the Republican states with that color.

The job of a historical researcher is like that of a detective. You have to examine the evidence, sift through accounts that often differ with one another, and try to determine the truth. Information is only as good as its source. If you don't know where the information comes from, it is of no value at all. I make no claims to this being a scholarly work. But even in a popular work of history, readers deserve to know the principal sources of the information, so that they can judge for themselves how good it is, and where to go to find out more. I've provided a story-by-story list with the selected sources for each.

This is the third in the *Greatest Stories* series of books, and with each one, more and more information is available via the Internet. There are some sites that I consulted so frequently that they deserve special mention. The *Encyclopaedia Britannica* (www.britannica.com) is a wonderful source for basic historical information. Wikipedia (www.wikipedia.com) proves more useful and accurate every year, although it is a good idea to double-check anything found there. The *New York Times* archive, available through many libraries, allows word searching of stories going back to 1857. The *Time* magazine archive (www.time.com) allows word searching of articles back to 1923. The Making of America Web site (http://cdl.library.cornell.edu/moa/) is a digital library of primary sources from the antebellum period through the early 1900s, including both books and magazines. I went back to each of these many, many times.

There are other terrific collections of primary sources on the Net. The Century of Lawmaking page on the Library of Congress Web site (http://memory.loc.gov/ammem/amlaw/lawhome.html) is a treasure trove of original documents pertaining to every session of Congress up until the 1870s. Also on the Library of Congress Web site is the George Washington Papers page, (http://memory.loc.gov/ammem/gwhtml/gwhome.html), the largest collection of original Washington documents in the world. And there are many other museums, universities, and other institutions amassing source material on the Internet, all within a click of your finger.

Even with all the Web has to offer, however, research still means hours spent with your nose in a book. Among the hundreds I looked at, there were several that proved particularly valuable. *To the Best of My Ability* by James McPherson provided a succinct overview of each and every American president. *The American Past*, more than sixty years after it was published, is still a wonderful romp through American history with illustrations on every page. I can extend to it the ultimate author's compliment: I wish I had written it. William Safire advised me to look for stories in his book *Safire's New Political Dictionary*. "It's a goddamn gold mine, Rick," were his exact words. He was right. Paul Boller's *Presidential Anecdotes* is a classic in the field, though some of the items in there should be taken with a grain of salt. For nailing down dates and other specifics, there's nothing like *Facts About the Presidents* by Joseph Nathan Kane.

History, though, is not just a set of facts, it is a conversation that has to be updated as new information becomes available and new interpretations are put forward. I encourage you to dig into the source material available and to take part in the conversation. If you find things that challenge the stories as told here, don't keep them to yourself. Please share. And when you discover other great stories that knock your socks off, let me know—I want to hear 'em! You can contact me via my Web site at www.rickbeyer.net.

Man Overboard!: *Of Plymouth Plantation* by William Bradford. *Ancestors of American Presidents* by Gary Boyd Roberts. MayflowerHistory.com (http://www.mayflowerhistory.com/Genealogy/famousdescendants.php).

Custody Battle: *Washington* by Douglas Southall Freeman. "Will of Lawrence Washington," Virginia Colonial Records Project.

The War of Jenkins' Ear: "Earmarked for War," by Jack Rudolph, *American History Illustrated*, February 1984. *A Brief History of the Caribbean* by Jan Rogozinski.

First President: *John Hanson, Our First President* by Seymour Weiss Smith. *The Patriot's Handbook* by George Grant.

Bible Blunder: "George Washington Swore Here," *Life*, Feb. 1989. "Footnote on the Masonic Bible Used in Inauguration" by Richard Pyle, Associated Press, Feb. 4, 2001. "I Swear: Last Minute Availability Puts Masons' Bible into History" by Patricia Zapor, Catholic News Service.

Title Trauma: *John Adams* by David McCullough. "Maclay's Journal," A Century of Lawmaking (http://memory.loc.gov/ammem/amlaw/lwmj.html). "Senate Journal," May 14, 1789, A Century of Lawmaking (http://memory.loc.gov/ammem/amlaw/lwsj.html). *To the Best of My Ability* by James McPherson.

House Hunting: "The White House, Plans Unrealized and Realized" by William Seale, in *Our Changing White House*, ed. Wendell Garrett. *Real Life at the White House* by John and Claire Whitcomb. National Building Museum (http://www.nbm.org).

Matchmaker: *Dolley Madison, Her Life and Times* by Katharine Anthony. *Strength and Honor: The Life of Dolley Madison* by Richard N. Cote.

Washington's Whiskey: The George Washington Papers at the Library of Congress (http://memory.loc.gov/ammem/gwhtml/gwhome.html). "George Washington Drank Here" by Jill Sim, *American Heritage*, Mar. 2004.

Pivotal Vote: *Adams vs. Jefferson: The Tumultuous Election of 1800* by John Ferling.

Jefferson Handshake: *A Treasury of White House Tales* by Webb Garrison. *Facts About the Presidents* by

Joseph Nathan Kane. *Real Life at the White House* by John and Claire Whitcomb. *The Rise of Roosevelt* and *Theodore Rex* by Edmund Morris.

The Gospel According to Thomas: *The Jefferson Bible* by Thomas Jefferson, with an introduction by Douglas E. Lurton.

Political Monster: *Facts About the Presidents* by Joseph Nathan Kane. *The American Past* by Roger Butterfield.

Jackson and Benton: *The Revolutionary Age of Andrew Jackson* by Robert V. Remini.

A Capital Idea: *The African-American Mosaic*, Library of Congress Resource Guide for the Study of Black History & Culture (http://www.loc.gov/exhibits/african/intro.html).

The Naked President: *Presidential Anecdotes* by Paul Boller. John Quincy Adams diary, June 13, 1825; part of the collections of Adams Family resources online at the Massachusetts Historical Society (http://www.masshist.org/adams/). E-mail note from Sara Sikes at the Massachusetts Historical Society, Oct. 3, 2006.

Dead Broke: *Strange and Fascinating Facts About Presidents* by Charles Reichblum. "Jefferson Gate (Thomas Jefferson and the Library of Congress)" by Art Plotnick, *American Libraries*, Dec. 1987. *Lost Pages of History* by Garrison Webb.

Masons, Morgan, and Murder: *Revolutionary Brotherhood* by Steve Bullock. *The Anti-Mason Party* by William Preston Vaughn.

The Petticoat Affair: *Parlor Politics* by Catherine Allgor. *The Revolutionary Age of Andrew Jackson* by Robert Remini. "Andrew Jackson's 'Petticoat Affair'" by J. Kingston Pierce, *American History*, June 1999.

The Bastard and the Brahmin: *The Stranger and the Statesman* by Nina Burleigh. "James Smithson, Founder of the Smithsonian Institution," Smithsonian Scrapbook, (http://siarchives.si.edu/history/exhibits/documents/smithson.html).

125,000 to One: *Plots Against Presidents* by John Mason Potter. *American Assassins* by James W. Clarke. "Political Assassination: The Violent Side of American Political Life," Digital History (http://www.digitalhistory.uh.edu/historyonline/assassinations.cfm).

Old Kinderhook: *Milestones in the History of English* by Allen Walker Read.

Having a Ball: *American Heritage Pictorial History of American Presidents*. *We the People: The American People and Their Government*.

The Power of Speech: *Plots Against Presidents* by John Mason Potter. *To The Best of My Ability* by James McPherson. Various articles in the *New York Times*, Oct. 15, 1912.

Lincoln's Duel: *The Astonishing Saber Duel of Abraham Lincoln* by James E. Myers. *Lincoln: The Prairie Years* by Carl Sandburg.

State Funeral: *Santa Anna: Napoleon of the West* by Frank Hanighen. "Antonio López de Santa Anna," New Perspectives on the West, PBS (http://www.pbs.org/weta/thewest/people/s_z/santaanna .html).

Hail to the Wives!: "Hail to the Chief," Patriotic Melodies (http://lcweb2.loc.gov/cocoon/ihas/loc .natlib.ihas.200000009/default.html). U.S. Marine Band (www.marineband.usmc).

Saved by a Song: *A Treasury of White House Tales* by Webb Garrison. "Fatal Cruise of the Princeton" by Ann Blackman, *Naval History*, September 2005.

Telegraph Hill: *Lightning Man: The Accursed Life of Samuel F. B. Morse* by Kenneth Silverman. "The First News Message by Telegraph" by John Kirk, from the files of the architect of the Capitol.

Mail Call: *Perley's Reminiscences* by Benjamin Perley Poore. *To the Best of My Ability* by James McPherson.

Short-Term Solution: "The President You Never Heard Of" by David Lester, Jan. 18, 1953, from the files of the Missouri Historical Encyclopedia. "President for a Day," United States Senate Art & History Home (http://www.senate.gov/artandhistory/history/minute/President_For_A_Day.html). This deadly serious article scoffs at the idea that Atchison was actually president, but does a terrific of job of laying out all the facts and arguments in great detail.

Patent President: *Lincoln: The Prairie Years* by Carl Sandburg. Abraham Lincoln Online.org (http:// www.abrahamlincolnonline.com).

Forgotten Fillmore: *Millard Fillmore* by Robert J. Scarry. *To the Best of My Ability* by James McPherson.

The Filibuster: *The Filibuster: The Career of William Walker* by Laurence Greene. "William Walker," in *Historic World Leaders*, ed. Anne Commir.

Buchanan's Blunder: *Declarations of Independence: The Encyclopedia of American Autonomist and Secessionist Movements* by James Erwin. "Utah War: US Government Versus Mormon Settlers," *Wild West* magazine, (http://www.historynet.com/magazines/wild_west/3033416.html). Various articles in the *New York Times* from 1857 and 1858.

A Touch of Grace: *Lincoln's Little Girl* by Fred Trump. Mr. Lincoln and New York, (http://www .mrlincolnandnewyork.org).

And Tyler Too?: *The Civil War* by Shelby Foote.

Where There's Smoke . . . : *The Civil War* by Shelby Foote.

Failed Speech: *Abraham Lincoln*, abridged, by Carl Sandburg. *The War for the Union* by Allan Nevins.

What Dreams May Come: *With Malice Toward None: A Life of Abraham Lincoln* by Stephen B. Oates. *History of the United States Secret Service* by Lafayette Charles Baker.

The Man Who Shot Booth: *Manhunt* by James Swanson. "Boston Corbett Hopelessly Insane," *New York Times*, Oct. 2, 1887.

The Jinx: *Robert Todd Lincoln: A Man in His Own Right* by James S. Goff.

The Man Who Saved the Presidency: *Profiles in Courage* by John F. Kennedy. *American Heritage Pictorial History of the Presidents of the United States*.

Speed Demon: *To the Best of My Ability* by James McPherson. The White House Historical Association (www.whitehousehistory.org). *Grant* by Jean Edward Smith.

The Buffalo Hangman: "When Grover Cleveland Acted as Hangman," *New York Times*, July 7, 1912.

Mrs. Satan: *The Woman Who Ran for President* by Lois Beachy Underhill. *Other Powers* by Barbara Goldsmith.

The Body Snatchers: "The Plot to Steal Lincoln's Body" by Deanne and Peggy Robertson, *American Heritage*, April/May 1982. "Bold Attempt to Rob the Tomb," *New York Times*, Nov. 9, 1876. "The Graveyard Robbers," *New York Times*, May 31, 1878.

The Editor and the Election: *Fraud of the Century* by Roy Morris Jr. "Death of John Reid," *New York Times*, Jan. 26, 1897. "Just What Chandler Did," *New York Times*, June 15, 1887.

Undercover Oath: *Fraud of the Century* by Roy Morris Jr. *Rutherford B. Hayes* by Harry Barnard.

Let the Good Times Roll: 2005 Easter Egg Roll, 〈http://www.whitehouse.gov/easter/2005/〉. History of the White House Easter Egg Roll (http://clinton2.nara.gov/WH/glimpse/Easter/). Various articles in the *New York Times*.

Assassination Tech: "1881—Garfield Shot" by Frederick D. Schwarz, *American Heritage,* June/July 2006. *Garfield* by Allan Peskin. *Reminiscences of an Astronomer* by Simon Newcomb. Various articles in the *New York Times*.

This Old House: *The President's House* by Margaret Truman. *President's House* by William Seale.

The Peabody Connection: "Who Was Wyatt Earp" by Allen Barra, *American Heritage*, Dec. 1998. "Victorian Headmaster," *Time*, Oct. 30, 1944.

And the Truth Will Set You Free: *To the Best of My Ability* by James McPherson. *Presidential Anecdotes* by Paul Boller.

Casting a Political Spell: *Why You Say It* by Webb Garrison. "A Spellbinding Affair," *New York Times*, Nov. 15, 1888. "Stabbed Him to Death," *New York Times*, Nov. 9, 1889.

Animal House: Various materials from the Presidential Pet Museum.

Secret Surgery: *The Shadow Presidents* by Michael Medved. "Secret Operation on Cleveland Told," *New York Times*, Feb. 20, 1932.

The Cutting Edge: *Blood: An Epic History of Medicine and Commerce* by Douglas Starr. "Red Gold," PBS, (http://www.pbs.org). "Carnot Killed," *New York Times*, June 25, 1984.

Labor Day: *Grover Cleveland* by Edwin P. Hoyt. *An Honest President* by Paul Jeffers. "People & Events: George Pullman, American Experience" (http://www.pbs.org/wgbh/amex/chicago/peopleevents/p_pullman.html). "Labor Day a National Holiday," *New York Times*, June 29, 1894. It is worth noting that most tellings of this story suggest Cleveland created the holiday after the strike was over, but in fact, he signed the bill into law while the strike was still on, and before he sent troops to Chicago.

Buttoned Up: *Instant Expert: Collecting Political Memorabilia* by Richard Friz. *Occupations for Women* by Frances Elizabeth Willard. "Political Pin Ups" by Neil Grauer, *Cigar Aficionado*, autumn 1996.

The President and the Priest: "Bulletproof Priest" by Paul Collins, *New Scientist*, April 23, 2005. *The Great Round World and What Is Going On in It*, vol. 1, no. 47, Sept. 30, 1897. Various articles in the *New York Times*.

Guess Who's Coming to Dinner?: *Theodore Rex* by Edmund Morris. *TR: The Last Romantic* by H. W. Brands. "Southern Democrats Berate the President," *New York Times*, Oct. 19, 1901.

Teddy Bear: *Timelab 2000*, written and produced by Rick Beyer for the History Channel.

Spellbound: *The Shadow Presidents* by Michael Medved. "The American Spelling Reform Movement" by Richard Whalen, *Verbatim*, autumn 2002. Various articles in the *New York Times*.

The Man Who Saved Football: *They Changed the Game* by Howard Liss. *TR: The Last Romantic* by H. W. Brands. *New York Times*, various articles in 1905 and 1906. "NCAA Born from Need to Bridge Football and Higher Education" by Kay Hawes, *NCAA News*, Nov. 8, 1999. Archival material provided by Saint Louis University.

Court of Appeal: *Nellie Taft: The Unconventional First Lady of the Ragtime Era* by Carl Sferrazza Anthony.

Presidential Phrasemaker: *Safire's New Political Dictionary* by William Safire. Materials supplied by the Tennessee Historical Society.

The Shape of the Presidency: *Real Life at the White House* by John and Claire Whitcomb. *The President's House* by Bess Truman. *Safire's New Political Dictionary* by William Safire.

You're Out!: *Baseball: The President's Game* by William B. Mead and Paul Dickson. Various articles in the *New York Times*.

First in the Nation: *Why New Hampshire? The First-in-the-Nation Primary State* by Hugh Gregg.

A Nickel for Your Thoughts: "What This Country Needs Is a Really Good 5-Cent Cigar" by Jeffrey Graft, Indiana Notes and Queries (http://www.indiana.edu/~librcsd/internet/extra/cigar.html). Various articles in *Time*.

Wartime Wool: Various articles in the *New York Times*. *America's First Families* by Carl Sferrazza Anthony.

Analyze This: *Thomas Woodrow Wilson: A Psychological Study* by William Bullitt and Sigmund Freud. "Freud and Bullitt Book Assails Wilson," *New York Times*, Nov. 30, 1966, as well as other articles from the *New York Times*.

Convoy: *At Ease* by Dwight D. Eisenhower. "Motor Traffic Needs Shown by Army Tour," *New York Times*, Oct. 26, 1919.

The Woman Who Became President: *Edith and Woodrow* by Phyllis Lee Levin. *A Treasury of White House Tales by* Webb Garrison.

Thank You for Smoking: *Safire's New Political Dictionary* by William Safire. "Col. George Harvey Dies in Dublin, NH," *New York Times*, Aug. 20, 1928.

The Talkative President: *The Talkative President: The Off-the-Record Press Conferences of Calvin Coolidge*, ed. Howard H. Quint and Robert H. Ferrell.

The Name Game: *Herbert Hoover and the Great Depression* by Harris Gaylord Warren. "But Is It History?" *Time*, Mar. 11, 1957. *Safire's New Political Dictionary* by William Safire.

Gotta Go!: *Lyndon Johnson and the American Dream* by Doris Kearns Goodwin. *Lyndon Johnson: Portrait of a President* by Robert Dallek.

The Business Plot: *Maverick Marine* by Hans Schmidt. "A Plot Without Plotters," *Time*, Dec. 3, 1934. *The Plot to Seize the White House* by Jules Archer.

Presidential Payoff: U.S. Treasury Web site (http://www.treas.gov/education/faq/currency/denominations.shtml). *Legacies: Collecting America's History at the Smithsonian* (http://www.smithsonianlegacies.si.edu/objectdescription.cfm?ID=29). Various articles in the *New York Times*.

Third-Rate Burglary: *Richard Nixon, American Politician* by Rachel Stiffler Barron. "The Young Richard Nixon," *Life*, Nov. 6, 1970.

Don't Mess with Thanksgiving: Clippings, letters, and memoranda on file at the Franklin D. Roosevelt Library, Hyde Park, New York.

Model J. Ford: *Time and Choice: Gerald Ford's Appointment with History* by James Cannon. *Cover Girls: The Story of Harry Conover* by Carole Conover. Various articles in the *New York Times*.

Lights On: "Baseball During World War II: The Reaction and Encouragement of Franklin Delano Roosevelt and Others" by Gerald Bazer and Steven Culbertson, *Nine,* fall 2001. Various articles in the *New York Times. Baseball: The President's Game* by William B. Mead and Paul Dickson.

Close Call of the *Porter:* "Torpedo on the Starboard Beam" by Commander Charles F. Pick Jr., Naval Institute Proceeding, Aug. 1970. *Affectionately, FDR* by James Roosevelt and Sidney Shalett. Log of President Roosevelt's trip aboard the USS *Iowa,* FDR Library. Author's interview with *William D. Porter* crew member Bob Jones.

Where Does It Stop?: Information from the Truman Presidential Library (www.trumanlibrary .org). *Truman* by David McCullough. *Safire's New Political Dictionary*, by William Safire.

Jack's First Wife: *The Dark Side of Camelot* by Seymour Hersh. "An American Genealogy," *Time*, Sept. 28, 1962.

First Debate: *Kennedy and Nixon* by Chris Matthews.

Makeup Moment: *The Making of the President, 1960* by Theodore White. *Tell Me a Story* by Don Hewitt.

Ich Bin Ein Berliner: Author interview with Robert Lochner on May 9, 2000. There is also a CNN interview on the Web site CNN Cold War (www.cnn.com/SPECIALS/cold.war/episodes/09/ reflections).

The Night the Lights Went On in Georgia: Jimmy Carter's original handwritten UFO report provided by the Carter Presidential Library. "Carter Once Saw a UFO on a 'Very Sober Occasion' " by Howell Raines, *Atlanta Constitution*, Sept. 14, 1973.

The King and I: Various primary source materials found on the National Security Archive (http:// www.gwu.edu/~nsarchiv/nsa/elvis/elnix.html).

Legacy Lost: *Shadow Presidents* by Michael Medved. (Medved's book was written in the late seventies, well before the Internet went public, and it is humorous in retrospect to see him take pains in pointing out all the ways he thinks the idea is just awful.) "Al Gore and the Creation of the Internet" by Richard Wiggins, First Monday (http://firstmonday.org/issues/issue5_10/wiggins/index.html).

Pandora's Box: *American Assassins* by James W. Clarke. Various articles in the *New York Times.*

Presidential Pardon: *Robert E. Lee* by Emory Thomas. "Robert E. Lee" by Gail Jarvis, LewRockwell. com.

The Code of the Secret Service: *Dutch* by Edmund Morris. Interview with Jerry Parr on *National Geographic* Web site. *The Secret Service* by Philip H. Melanson with Peter F. Stevens.

Anatomy of a Great Line: *It's My Party* by Peter Robinson.

Old Man's Vote: Various newspaper accounts of Mandela's election in 1994.

Seeing Red and Blue: "One State, Two State, Red State, Blue State" by Tom Zeller, *New York Times*, Feb. 8, 2004. Author's observation of various networks' election night coverage from 1956 to 2000, courtesy of the Museum of Broadcasting, New York. "Elephants are Red, Donkeys are Blue" by Paul Farhi, *Washington Post*, Nov. 2, 2004. Various articles in *Time* and the *New York Times*.

ACKNOWLEDGMENTS

On December 16, 1997, a pigeon dropped a bomb load on my shoulder as I was walking down East Forty-fifth Street in New York toward the offices of THE HISTORY CHANNEL. Distressed as I was by this unprovoked attack, it turned out to be a good omen. The meeting that followed (after I wiped off the pigeon mess) led to my working on the Timelab 2000 series of history minutes, which in turn led to my series of Greatest Stories Never Told books, of which this is the third. So perhaps I should begin the acknowledgments by thanking the pigeon.

I owe a greater debt of gratitude to Artie Scheff, who hired me to produce the Timelab series, and to the talented group of people who made that project a success. I've said it before, but it is worth saying again: their efforts laid the groundwork for these books.

Jacqueline Sheridan, my collaborator on half a dozen documentaries, has contributed to this book in various ways. She assisted in photo research, acted as a willing springboard for testing stories, and was a calming influence at times I was freaking out. Jacqueline, to answer the question you know I don't want to hear: Yes, I'm happy. Thanks also to Elizabeth Dougherty for her able help searching for stories.

Many presidential libraries offered invaluable help, especially the Truman Library, the Kennedy Library, the Ford Library, and the Carter Library. (A special tip of the hat to Sara Saunders at the Carter

Library and William McNitt at the Ford Library, who both came up with wonderful story suggestions I used.) I would also like to thank the Massachusetts Historical Society, the James Monroe Foundation, and the James Buchanan Foundation.

The National Archives and the Library of Congress are two invaluable national treasures. Any author looking to illustrate American history with archival photographs and maps knows what amazing resources these are, and over the years their staff members (yes, government employees all) have proved to be extraordinarily knowledgeable and unfailingly pleasant to deal with.

While talking about libraries, I wouldn't want to leave out the Carey Memorial Library in Lexington, Massachusetts, where the librarians are always gracious and helpful.

Help came from many sources. Ambassador Yrjö Länsipuro and press counselor Kristiina Helenius from the Finnish embassy in Washington offered valuable insight about what "Hoover" means in Finnish. Secret Service archivist Mike Sampson tracked down information I couldn't find anyplace else. Bob Jones and Bob Lochner were kind enough to share personal experiences that made it into these pages.

There's an old story about a hack actor who was booed while performing Shakespeare. "Why are you booing me?" he asked. "I didn't write this stuff." Well, I did write this stuff, but it took a bunch of other talented people to turn it into a book. Among them: Leah Carlson-Stanisic, who created the interior design; Judith Stagnitto Abbate, who laid out the pages; copy editor Chuck Antony; Yucca Design, who did the cover; and production editor Amy Vreeland.

The publication of this book marks several bittersweet partings. My agent, Arielle Eckstut of the Levine Greenberg Literary Agency, is leaving the agent business to pursue her dream in the world of online sock sales. (I'm not kidding!) Associate editor Joelle Yudin at HarperCollins also left to pursue other things midway through this book, although Jennifer Schulkind has ably stepped in.

This is the third book I've worked on with executive editor Mauro DiPreta. Mauro works with a lot of celebrity authors—and then there's me. Everybody enjoys some slumming once in a while. All kidding aside, working with him has been a rewarding experience. He fights like hell to make every part of the book as good as it can be, and to get it out there with the biggest push possible—what more can you ask? I hope we get to do many more projects together.

Finally, there is my wife, Marilyn. Paltry words of thanks are not enough to compensate for all she has done to help in the creation of these books. (Not to mention all the love she has showered on the author the past quarter century.) It would take another book to catalog her contributions. Emotional support, insightful comments, practical suggestions, gentle criticisms, and the occasional rap on the knuckles are just a few of the forms her help has taken. Without Marilyn, I doubt that I would have gotten through one book, never mind three. Thank you, darling.

Unless otherwise noted, photo credits for each page are listed top to bottom, and images are listed only the first time they appear. Credits for pages not listed can be found on the facing page. Every effort has been made to correctly attribute all the materials reproduced in this book. If any errors have been made, we will be happy to correct them in future editions.

Page x: author. **Page 1:** Painting by Mike Haywood; © CORBIS. **Pages 2–3:** LOC (all). **Page 4:** LOC, Mary Evans Picture Library. **Page 5:** LOC, author. **Page 6:** NARA, LOC. **Page 8:** LOC; © CORBIS. **Page 9:** LOC, Bible from St. John's Lodge #1, A.Y.M, F. & A.M., which is the custodian of it. **Pages 10–11:** LOC (all). **Page 12:** Maryland Historical Society; LOC. **Page 13:** Photo of Leinster House by Mick Quinn; LOC. **Pages 14–15:** LOC (all). **Page 16:** LOC. **Page 17:** Courtesy of the Mount Vernon Ladies Association. **Pages 18–19:** LOC (all). **Page 20:** LOC; David Roth. **Page 21:** author. **Page 22:** LOC; SI. **Pages 24–29:** LOC (all). **Page 30:** Art Resource; LOC. **Page 32:** LOC. **Page 33:** NARA. **Page 34:** National Heritage Museum; LOC. **Page 35:** LOC. **Pages 36–37:** LOC (all). **Page 38:** SI. **Page 39:** LOC. **Page 40:** LOC; SI. **Page 41:** LOC. **Page 42:** LOC. **Page 43:** LOC; University of Hartford. **Page 44:** author; LOC. **Page 45:** LOC. **Page 46:** LOC. **Page 47:** LOC; SI. **Page 48:** LOC. **Page 49:** Lincoln-Herndon Building Publishers, LOC. **Page 50:** LOC. **Page 51:** Illinois State Military Museum. **Pages 52–53:** LOC (all except for sheet music); United States Marine Corps Band. **Page 54:** Navy Military History Center; LOC. **Page 55:** LOC. **Pages 56–59:** LOC (all). **Page 60:** © CORBIS; Michael Reed. **Page 61:** LOC. **Page 62:** SI; United States Patent Office. **Page 63:** Thomas Jefferson Foundation. **Pages 64–67:** LOC (all). **Page 68:** © CORBIS; LOC. **Page 69:** © CORBIS. **Pages 70–71:** Detroit Public Library (all except Lincoln); LOC. **Pages 72–73:** LOC (all). **Pages 74–75:** LOC (all except Grant with cigar); © CORBIS. **Pages 76–77:** NARA (all except speech); LOC. **Pages 78–79:** LOC (all). **Page 80:** LOC; © CORBIS. **Pages 82–83:** LOC (all). **Pages 84–85:** LOC (all). **Pages 86–87:** New York Historical Society (carriage); LOC (all others). **Pages 88–89:** © CORBIS (noose); LOC (all others). **Pages 90–95:** LOC (all). **Page 96:** LOC. **Page 97:** Rutherford B. Hayes Presidential Center; LOC. **Page 98:** LOC. **Page 99:** LOC; © CORBIS. **Page 100:** Mary Evans

Picture Library. **Page 101:** LOC; author. **Page 102:** LOC. **Page 103:** Harry S. Truman Library; LOC. **Page 104:** LOC; Groton School. **Page 105:** © CORBIS (Earp); LOC; Groton School. **Pages 106–109:** LOC (all). **Page 110:** © CORBIS; LOC. **Page 111:** LOC. **Page 112:** Navy Military History Center; © CORBIS. **Page 113:** LOC. **Page 114:** LOC. **Page 115:** Getty Images; LOC. **Pages 116–117:** LOC (all). **Page 117:** author. **Page 118:** United States Patent Office. **Page 120:** © CORBIS; *New York Times*; **Page 121:** Brooklyn Public Library; LOC. **Page 122:** SI; LOC. **Page 123:** LOC. **Page 124:** Sagamore Hill National Historic Site; LOC. **Page 125:** SI. **Page 126:** LOC; Theodore Roosevelt Collection, Harvard College Library. **Page 127:** LOC. **Page 128:** Yale University. **Page 129:** *New York Times*; St. Louis University. **Pages 130–131:** LOC (except tub); Culver Pictures. **Page 132:** Tennessee Historical Society; LOC. **Page 133:** LOC. **Page 134:** LOC; NARA. **Page 135:** NARA; LOC. **Page 136:** Dwight D. Eisenhower Presidential Library and Museum; LOC. **Page 138:** Lyndon Baines Johnson Library and Museum; © CORBIS. **Page 139:** Bob LaPree; New Hampshire Primary Library. **Page 140:** John F. Kennedy Presidential Library and Museum; LOC. **Page 141:** John F. Kennedy Presidential Library and Museum; LOC. **Pages 142–145:** Library of Congress. **Pages 146–147:** Dwight D. Eisenhower Presidential Library and Museum (all except map); LOC (route added by author). **Pages 148–149:** LOC (all). **Page 150:** LOC. **Page 151:** © CORBIS; LOC. **Page 152:** Calvin Coolidge Presidential Library and Museum; LOC. **Page 153:** LOC. **Pages 154–155:** LOC (all). **Page 156:** © CORBIS; Lyndon Baines Johnson Library and Museum. **Page 157:** LOC; Lyndon Baines Johnson Library and Museum. **Pages 158–159:** LOC (all). **Pages 160:** SI. **Page 161:** United States Treasury. **Page 162:** CORBIS; LOC. **Page 163:** Duke University Archives. **Pages 164–165:** Franklin D. Roosevelt Presidential Library and Museum (all). **Pages 166–167:** Gerald R. Ford Presidential Library and Museum. (*Cosmopolitan* cover used with permission of *Cosmopolitan*.) **Page 168:** LOC. **Page 169:** National Baseball Hall of Fame; White House Association. **Pages 170–171:** NARA (all). **Page 172:** Harry S. Truman Presidential Library and Museum. **Page 173:** LOC; Harry S. Truman Museum and Library. **Page 174:** NARA. **Page 175:** LOC. **Page 176:** McKeesport Heritage Foundation; © CORBIS. **Page 177:** John. F. Kennedy Presidential Library and Museum. **Page 178–179:** © CORBIS (all). **Page 180:** author; Associated Press. **Page 181:** John F. Kennedy Presidential Library and Museum. **Page 182:** LOC; Jimmy Carter Library and Museum. **Pages 184–185:** NARA (all). **Page 186:** Courtesy of Len Kleinrock; NARA. **Page 187:** NARA. **Page 188:** LOC; © CORBIS. **Page 189:** © CORBIS; LOC. **Page 190:** Gerald R. Ford Presidential Library and Museum. **Page 191:** LOC. **Page 192:** Ronald Reagan Presidential Foundation and Library; author. **Page 193:** author. **Page 194–195:** Ronald Reagan Presidential Foundation and Library. **Pages 196–197:** © CORBIS (all). **Page 198:** University of Massachusetts Boston. **Page 199:** ©2006 NBC Universal, Inc. All Rights Reserved.